A WOMAN'S PLACE?

A WOMAN'S PLACE?

Leadership in the Church

C. S. COWLES

Beacon Hill Press of Kansas City
Kansas City, Missouri

Copyright 1993
by Beacon Hill Press of Kansas City

ISBN: 083-411-464X

Printed in the
United States of America

Cover Design: Crandall Vail

10 9 8 7 6 5 4 3 2 1

To
Lavernia May (deceased) and Milton Samuel Cowles,
Partners in Ministry,
To whom I owe my biological existence and my life in Christ.

CONTENTS

PREFACE

"Every good and perfect gift is from above, coming down from the Father of the heavenly lights" (James 1:17, NIV). The truth of this verse has been validated in my experience in that I cannot imagine myself having written this kind of book even a decade ago. Like Moses, whose attention was seized by a bush that burned without being consumed, I found myself taken quite by surprise in regard to the question of women in professional ministry. Through strange and wonderful providence, this issue has broken in upon my consciousness with a compelling force that will not let me go. One cannot easily shrug off that kind of divine inheritance.

Even so, I doubt that this book would have been written had not Dr. Wesley Tracy, editor of the *Herald of Holiness,* taken the initiative to forward a paper I had written to the Book Committee of the Church of the Nazarene, "Paul's Attitude Toward Women in Ministry." The committee, in turn, encouraged me to continue research and present in book form a biblical defense of women in ministry. It was their invitation that spurred me to pursue it. The project became, for me, an incredible journey into the joy of discovery.

I soon became aware, as I began my research, that the issues addressed have a far wider scope than the Church of the Nazarene. The place of women in the church continues to be one of the most debated, and divisive, questions in the greater church world today, particularly among Evangelicals. Though my personal context and point of departure is from within the Wesleyan theological tradition, my mission is to challenge those who take seriously the inspiration and authority of the Bible as the Word of God, to rework their exegesis and rethink their interpretation of scriptural teaching regarding the status of women, particularly those who are "in Christ Jesus" (Gal. 3:28).

I would like to thank my wife, Marge, and my children, for their unfailing encouragement and helpful critique. Also, my colleagues in the Division of Philosophy and Religion at Northwest Nazarene College have afforded me invaluable support and insights. I am deeply indebted to Bonnie Perry and Linda Quanstrom for their enthusiasm for the book and for their rigorous editing. I must also pay tribute to a vast community of biblical scholars, past and present, from whose work I have freely drawn.

INTRODUCTION

Melody, one of our senior preministerial majors and departmental teaching assistants, threw herself into a chair in my office, obviously upset. "Read this," she said, as she thrust a letter toward me. It was written on Church of the Nazarene stationery, signed by the secretary of the District Board of Ministerial Credentials. In one short, terse paragraph it said, "We regret to inform you that your request for a District Preacher's License has been denied." There was no invitation to reapply at some future date. The issue, as far as they were concerned, was settled.

I glanced up at Melody. She was biting her clenched fist. Her cheeks were wet with tears. I asked her to tell me about her interview with the board. She shared that her answers to questions relative to her Christian experience, her ministerial service, and her grasp of the doctrines of the church seemed to be well-received. When the interview was almost over, however, one of the pastors asked, "Why do you really want to be a preacher?"

"Because God has called me," she responded.

"Perhaps what you need," he countered, "is to marry a preacher." That remark elicited some chuckles, and it broke her heart. Obviously, they could not understand why a woman would want to enter into a profession that was so traditionally male-dominated.

Melody was an exceptional student with extraordinary gifts for ministry. She spent one summer working in an inner-city mission in Washington, D.C. The following summer she served as a youth intern in a small rural church, where she inherited one teenager. By summer's end, however, she had built the youth group to more than a dozen active participants. If there had ever been a woman with the gifts and grace to make a significant contribution to the church in professional ministry, it was Melody.

I was embarrassed for my colleagues on the credentials board who, apparently, had allowed their male chauvinism to blind them to this young woman's potential for ministry and had made them forgetful of the enormous contribution women ministers have made to our denomination throughout its history. I apologized to her for them and reassured her of our faith in her. I believed that she possessed the gifts, grace, and temperament to be a productive and fruitful minister in the church. I assured her that, in due season, the church would recognize God's call upon her life and give her its official blessing. I prayed with her before she left.

A thunderhead of righteous indignation began building in me over the insensitivity of those male ministers to a gifted young woman's sense of calling and self-esteem. Then I began to ask myself some searching questions: If I had been on that credentials board, would I have raised my voice in reproof of those who made light of her call? Would I have risen to her defense? What was my record like across 15 years of pastoral ministry? How many women ministers did I call to fill my pulpit as evangelists and guest speakers? In seeking for associates, did I even consider the possibility of a woman being on staff? How were potential women ministers and leaders to sense God's call if they never saw women preaching or teaching or exercising congregational leadership in my churches? In 15 years, was there even one woman called to full-time ministry because of my preaching and encouragement?

How proactive was I in encouraging women to discover and exercise their spiritual gifts in the church? How often did I invite women to read the Scriptures or pray in public worship services? Or even take up the offering?

Women far outnumbered men in the active membership of every church I pastored. Yet, how sensitive was I that they be granted equal representation on the boards and committees of the church?

While I never considered myself to be antifeminist, on reflection, I had to admit that, like most ministers of my generation within the evangelical movement, I had unself-consciously drifted along in the traditionalist stream of patriarchal hierarchy where men are the dominant players and women comprise the supporting cast. I was embarrassed when I thought back over all the sermons I had preached that only reinforced the stereotype of dominant husbands and submissive wives, insensitive to the fact that many, if not most, of the women in my churches were unmarried, divorced, or had non-Christian husbands. I asked myself: Had I ever encouraged women to claim their full inheritance under God, as bearers of His divine image, who calls them to be who they are in their own right quite apart from whether or not they are married? Had I made a conscious effort to help them discover and exercise any spiritual gifts other than that of being a wife and homemaker? What had I ever said to the majority of women in my churches who were not presently actively mothering? Had I affirmed them as having full status before God, in their own right, or usefulness in the church apart from teaching Sunday School, singing in the choir, and serving covered-dish dinners? When I began to soberly assess my own nonsensitivity to women, my edifice of indignation against my colleagues collapsed. I found myself repeating the words of the spiritual, "It's me, it's me, O Lord,/Standing in the need of prayer."

Then I began to think about the enormous impact women ministers had made upon my life. I remember calling out for my mother, a nonordained but productive woman preacher-teacher, to come and pray with me as a 13-

year-old under terrible conviction. She knelt beside my bed and took my hands into hers. Her gentle prayer helped me across the great divide from fear and condemnation to faith and security in Jesus Christ. Shortly thereafter, I heard a woman evangelist preach. I was amused by her keen sense of humor, astonished at her lively pulpit antics, and convicted by her preaching. It was at the close of one of her sermons that I knelt at my pew and surrendered my life to the Lordship of Jesus.

Then I thought about Janet, a single Presbyterian missionary, who led a Sunday afternoon Christian Endeavor group for English-speaking teens in Hong Kong where my parents served as missionaries. Even today, I can see her face light up like that of an angel as she spoke of Jesus. Her Christlike spirit and gentle manner made an indelible impression on me. Working in that same mission was a Presbyterian couple where both preached. I recall distinctly being more enthralled by her sermons than by his.

A parade of women ministers, including evangelists, marched across the screen of my mind, along with a host of gifted women educators who taught me in college and formed the backbone of the churches I pastored. Two books that exploded like bombshells in my mind, greatly impacting the development of my theology and preaching in my formative years, were written by women: Catherine Marshall's *Beyond Ourselves* and Mildred Bangs Wynkoop's *Theology of Love*. Across nearly two decades of teaching Bible and theology in two colleges, many of my most gifted and capable preministerial students have been women. Sadly, they have met passive resistance on the part of a male-dominated church and, like Melody, have failed to receive the kind of official sanction or open doors necessary for the exercise and development of their gifts and calling. Few are serving the church today in professional ministerial roles, and to my knowledge none are senior pastors.

I had to candidly admit that I was more a part of the problem than a part of the answer. In spite of the enormous impact women ministers, theologians, and leaders had made on my life, I, too, had endorsed the prevailing evangelical philosophy of church growth that deliberately builds upon male leadership. I, too, had allowed the revolution in contemporary society regarding women's liberation to pass me by, unnoticed and unaffected, except to occasionally lash out at the "feminists" whom I believed were undermining traditional values and were contributing to the destruction of families. I refused to really listen to what they were saying about the gross inequities under which women have suffered since the dawn of world history. I, too, had allowed myself to be squeezed into the mold of Evangelicalism's blatantly sexist opposition to women's equal rights in church and society.

Several weeks after Melody laid that disturbing letter on my desk, she came bounding into my office, excitement radiating from her face. "Guess what," she announced. "My pastor just called me and asked if I would preach for him while home on spring break." Although she had taught Sunday School classes and had preached dozens of informal sermons to mission crowds and youth groups, this was her first invitation to preach for a regular service in a local church from behind a pulpit. She preached the sermon she had submitted to me for our college's senior sermon contest. Not only her numerous relatives but also many in the small town who had watched her grow up came to hear Melody preach. They were not disappointed. Early the next morning, while she and some friends were making the long drive back to the college, their car hit an antelope and rolled off the road. Melody was killed.

Several weeks after this tragic accident, I received the sermons entered by 27 preministerial students back from the judges. I added up their scores. Melody's sermon tied for first place. As a finalist, she would have preached it before the entire student body, if she had lived. Her text was:

> Though the fig tree does not blossom,
>> and no fruit is on the vines;
> though the produce of the olive fails
>> and the fields yield no food;
> though the flock is cut off from the fold
>> and there is no herd in the stalls,
> yet I will rejoice in the Lord;
>> I will exult in the God of my salvation.
> God, the Lord, is my strength;
>> he makes my feet like the feet of a deer,
>> and makes me tread upon the heights.
>
>>>> (Hab. 3:17-19)

Melody's death affected me profoundly. After much soul-searching, I determined that I could no longer drift along passively with the prevailing traditionalist tide. Though her voice was silenced, mine was not. I would speak for her and on behalf of all who, like her, are making a concerted effort to respond to the call of God to preach. I would become proactive in encouraging women to preach and exercise their spiritual gifts in public ministry. I would do everything possible to sensitize the church concerning its unique and glorious heritage of inclusiveness and equality.

Furthermore, I would call upon the church to open its pulpits, lecterns, and boardrooms to whomever the Holy Spirit should call and whomever evidenced gifts for public ministry, without regard to race, social class, or gender. It is time for the church to rediscover the richness, beauty, and spiritual power that can be released only through the full expression of women's unique gifts and special sensitivities. To this end this book is dedicated.

"In Christ Jesus you are all
children of God through faith.
As many of you as were baptized into Christ
have clothed yourselves with Christ.
**There is no longer Jew or Greek,
there is no longer slave or free,
there is no longer male and female;
for all of you are one in Christ Jesus."**

(GAL. 3:26-28, emphasis added)

· 1

The Fractured Church

*T*he greatest social revolution in the history of humankind has occurred in this century. It is not so much the scientific, nor technological, nor any political revolution, but rather the radical change in the status of women relative to men. Possibilities have exploded for women today that their great-grandmothers could scarcely have imagined. They have been granted, by law, all of the rights and privileges that have been traditionally the exclusive province of men. They have a voice and a vote in every public assembly. They have access to education in all fields of human inquiry. They have found open doors in all occupations and every profession. They have distinguished themselves as educators, authors, artists, administrators, executives, scientists, researchers, engineers, pilots, astronauts, physicians, attorneys, performers, reporters, newscasters, and judges. They have served ably in Congress, as governors, on the Supreme Court, and as heads of state.

For the first time in human history women, in Western civilization, have achieved full equality and relative parity with men in virtually every area of society—**except the church!** The church remains—with few exceptions—**the last bastion of institutional discrimination against wom-**

en. Women, for instance, continue to be locked out of the priesthood and positions of authority in the Roman Catholic church, as well as all branches of the Eastern Orthodox churches.

The Southern Baptist church, Protestantism's largest denomination—with nearly 100,000 churches and over 14 million members—passed a resolution at its 1984 general convention in Kansas City, calling upon local congregations to abide by the tradition of male leadership in ministry. As a result, it has been almost impossible for approximately 600 women, currently ordained as ministers by local Baptist churches, to function in official ministerial roles, according to Mary Zimmer, executive director of Southern Baptist Women in Ministry. They have tried to find an outlet for their call as institutional chaplains, youth ministers, directors of Christian education, educators in Christian colleges, and foreign missionaries. The Association of Southern Baptist Women in Ministry, organized in 1983, has been repeatedly denied any official status within the denomination and has been denied opportunity to meet during its general conventions, says Zimmer.[1]

On October 18, 1987, the Prescott Memorial Baptist Church in Memphis made a move that sent a shock wave rippling through the Southern Baptist denomination. They called Rev. Nancy Sehested as their pastor. She was one of the first female pastors in their history and the first to gain national media attention. The reaction to this novel move was swift and decisive. Four hundred male delegates of the Shelby Baptist Association, which represented 120 churches in the Memphis area, promptly met behind closed doors and expelled the congregation from its association. Another regional association in Tennessee recently threatened the expulsion of a congregation that merely considered opening its board of deacons to women.

The net result of this open and blatant discrimination against women is that the Body of Christ continues to suffer a seismic fracture of cosmic dimensions. While the walls between "Jew and Gentile" have been torn down and the chasm between "bond and free" has been bridged, the Body of Christ is not yet all "one in Christ Jesus" (Gal. 3:28). The "great divide" sundering the church is gender driven. Women, who constitute the majority of members in every church, are second-class citizens. They are denied access to pulpits, lecterns, and boardrooms for no other reason than their gender. Women ministers, in particular, feel the sting of rejection and exclusion. Diane Cunningham Leclerc, a senior pastor in the Church of the Nazarene, shares her experience: "Even if I might want to 'hang out' with the ministerial association that labels itself as 'evangelical,' I am not welcome because some of the dear brothers won't associate with a woman pastor for 'biblical' reasons. They don't want to appear as if they condone such a thing as me!"[2]

It is surely more than strange—even scandalous—that the very church that professes, with the apostle Paul, to be "the true circumcision, who worship in the Spirit of God and glory in Christ Jesus and **put no confidence in the flesh**" (Phil. 3:3, NASB, emphasis added), nevertheless makes the flesh the decisive criteria determining access to professional ministry. Natural talent and spiritual gifts, even a divine call to preach, are rendered null and void on the basis of human physiology.

There is, however, a small but mighty movement of churches that have historically taken strong exception to such flagrant gender discrimination. From their various beginnings, holiness churches in the Wesleyan-Arminian tradition have granted women all of the rights and privileges of membership, ministry, and leadership that are accorded to men. For example, during the first quarter century of the Church of the Nazarene's history, over 20 percent of its pastors, evangelists, and missionaries were ordained women. In some regions, as recently as the decades of the 1930s and 1940s, as many as 30 to 40 percent of its preachers were women. Women have served with distinction as pastors, evangelists, missionaries, educators, theologians, Bible scholars, counselors, scholars, authors, administrators, board members, and local leaders. As recently as its 1980 General Assembly, the Church of the Nazarene reemphasized its historic position in regard to women in ministry by affirming: "We support the right of women to use their God-given spiritual gifts within the church. We affirm the historic right of women to be elected and appointed to places of leadership within the Church of the Nazarene. We oppose any legislation which would be against the scriptural teachings of the place of womanhood in society."[3]

The enfranchisement of women in the holiness tradition has been based upon a settled conviction that the dispensation of the Holy Spirit has dawned, empowering both men and women to declare the unsearchable riches of Christ as prophesied by Joel and proclaimed by Peter on the Day of Pentecost:

In the last days it will be, God declares,
that I will pour out my Spirit upon all flesh,
and your sons **and your daughters** shall prophesy,
and your young men shall see visions,
and your old men shall dream dreams.
Even upon my slaves, **both men and women,**
in those days I will pour out my Spirit;
and they shall prophesy.
(Acts 2:17-18, emphasis added)

In the last few decades, however, there has been a decided erosion of this distinctive heritage in the Church of the Nazarene. Only 12.8 percent of licensed ministers (327 out of 2,564) are women, and only 4 percent (377 out of 9,394) are ordained elders (1992 statistics). Sixty-five women are presently serving as senior pastors (less than 1 percent of churches), and 134 serve as staff ministers. Nineteen are registered as evangelists. Fifty-two percent of licensed and ordained women are either unassigned or retired.[4] A sister denomination, the Church of God (Anderson, Ind.) reports the same shrinkage, from 32 percent of their congregations led by women pastors to less than 3 percent by 1975.[5]

No women have ever been elected to the general superintendency or as directors of the five divisions that oversee the Church of the Nazarene's various ministries. Only two women presently serve as district superintendents, one in the Philippines and the second in the Caribbean. Only one woman has ever served as a district superintendent in North America, and then only for part of a year until a suitable male minister could be elected.[6] No Nazarene institution of higher learning in the United States has ever had a woman president, and few have women represented on their board of trustees. Religion faculties are overwhelmingly male.

Even though women comprise the majority of members in local churches, they are a distinct minority on most church boards. In some local churches they have been denied leadership positions by congregational vote or pastoral edict. District superintendents seldom recommend women as pastors or associates. They protest that their hands are tied in that churches are unwilling to consider women candidates. The few who serve as staff ministers usually function in children's or women's ministries. Worship leadership in church services, conventions, and assemblies is invariably male. Rarely are women called upon to read Scripture, pray, lead congregational singing, administer the sacraments, or even serve as ushers.

Why such retrenchment? While holiness churches have given theological assent to equality, they nevertheless have generally accepted, implicitly and uncritically, cultural patriarchy as the "biblical" norm. Permitting women to preach or serve in positions of leadership has not signalled a change in this traditional hierarchy but has only stretched the boundaries to accommodate those exceptional women who have been aggressive and assertive enough to make their voices heard. Women preachers have generally been more tolerated than welcomed, even in the best of times. Their biographies and letters indicate that they constantly faced entrenched male chauvinism, both outside the church and at all levels within. They have had few male champions and even fewer female. What ministry they have exercised, they have invariably carved out for themselves as evangelists, educators, missionaries, and church planters. Rarely have women been called to pastor strong churches or been elected to lead established denominational organizations.

Another potent factor is the pervasive influence of the larger evangelical movement with its powerful media outlets. It has consistently and redundantly promoted patriarchal hierarchy in church and home as being the only biblically defensible tradition. It has mounted the most vocal and virulent backlash against the contemporary feminist movement, for which it blames most of the ills afflicting marriages and families today. Equal rights for women is viewed not as desirable but as deplorable. It is seen as a threat to "traditional family values" and a violation of "biblical principles." When members of holiness churches are made aware of their own church's history of openness to women in ministry, many are openly nonsupportive, and even ashamed, of their heritage. And why should they behave differently, not hearing or reading a strong, biblically based apologetic for women preachers and equality in male-female relationships, and not seeing credible models of women in active ministerial roles?[7] Consequently, another of the "distinctives" of holiness tradition has been all but lost.

Early Pentecostals welcomed and endorsed women as ministers. In recent decades, however, women have experienced the same exclusion from leadership roles as has been true in holiness churches. While they are tolerated and even encouraged as "prophesying daughters"—particularly as evangelists and missionaries—they are usually denied institutional presence as pastors or denominational leaders. Prominent charismatic ministers have been as opposed to women in authority as any other opponents of women ministers.[8]

Most of the mainline denominations have officially, although belatedly, opened the door to women for ordination. Yet it has been difficult, if not impossible, for women to exercise their ministry on a par equal with men. When it comes to positions of authority, it is still a man's world except for the occasional token woman, such as Barbara Harris, who in 1990 became the first female bishop in the Episcopal church, an event unprecedented in the 450-year history of the Anglican church—not to mention nearly 2,000 years of Anglo-Catholic history. Yet even on the historic occasion of her consecration, the service was rudely interrupted by Rev. James Cupid, Jr., an Episcopal priest of the Diocese of New York, who issued a formal objection. He implored the presiding bishop to halt proceedings, saying that he believed "her consecration and election were contrary to sound doctrine and the consecration an intractable impediment to the realization of that visible unity of the church for which Christ prayed."[9]

Another example can be cited. Lutheran theologian Philip J. Hefner protested, in the 1960s, that the role of women in the Lutheran church was their greatest scandal and hidden problem. The Lutheran Church in America responded by being the first of the Lutheran bodies to grant ordination to women in 1970. It appeared that gender walls had been breached when, in 1982, a number of women were elected to serve on a commission of 70 Lutherans to form a new Lutheran church, which became the Evangelical Lutheran Church in America. Yet, when it came to choosing its leadership, of the 65 new bishops appointed, not one was a woman. Only one was elected to head a major denominational division, and she was chosen, predictably, to lead the women's commission.[10]

A similar situation exists in the Presbyterian church. Elizabeth Howell Verdesi published a book titled *In but Still Out* (1973). In it she concludes that while women have achieved ecclesiastical equality and have been given significant responsibility in both lay and clergy roles, they are still marginalized. She described this situation as one of "being *in* but still *out* of the central currents of the church."[11]

So it goes for officials in the National Council of Churches. Champions of social justice and nondiscrimination, they nevertheless maintain a male-dominated lock on positions of power and prestige. Only one woman has been elected to fill the position of general secretary, and she was not ordained. The council lists no woman as head of a member communion. Likewise, the World Council of Churches, which, for all of its egalitarian pronouncements, has yet to elect a woman to any of its major offices.[12]

Gender discrimination in the church is rigorously defended on biblical grounds. The Council on Biblical Manhood and Womanhood, whose members comprise a who's who list of evangelical leaders (Bill Bright, Jerry Falwell, Carl F. H. Henry, Beverly La Haye, et al.), recently published the "Danvers Statement" in *Christianity Today*. It summarizes their position in this way: "We are convinced that Scripture affirms male leadership in the home, and that in the church certain governing and teaching roles are restricted to men. . . . Both Old and New Testaments . . . affirm the principle of male headship in the family and in the covenant community."[13]

This council arose as a reaction against the erosion of traditional roles of male dominance and female subordination in church and home, due largely—in their judgment—to the encroachment of a secular humanist-feminist view of equality. It originated in response to "the emergence of roles for men and women in church leadership that do not conform to Biblical teaching" and "the increasing prevalence and acceptance of hermeneutical oddities devised to reinterpret apparently plain meanings of Biblical texts."[14]

Which texts? The first cited is the creation story where Adam is created first, and then Eve as his "helper" (Gen. 2:18; see vv. 4-25). This is believed to represent the "order of creation" by which patriarchal hierarchy is established as a divinely ordained and immutable institution. Since the Genesis story of the Fall focuses attention almost exclusively upon Eve, the one deceived, she is blamed for the entrance of sin into the world (Genesis 3). The subsequent curse directed to Eve, and to all her female descendants, declares that "your desire shall be for your husband, **and he shall rule over you**" (v. 16, emphasis added). Paul seems not only to accept but also to affirm an ironclad subordination of women to men when he writes, "But I want you to understand that Christ is the head of every man, and the husband is the head of his wife, and God is the head of Christ. . . . he [man] is the image and reflection of God; but woman is the reflection of man. Indeed, man was not made from woman, but woman from man. Neither was man created for the sake of woman, but woman for the sake of man" (1 Cor. 11:3, 7-9).

The hierarchy of male domination and female subordination is given further support in Paul's command to the churches at Ephesus and Colossae: "Wives, be subject to your husbands as you are to the Lord. For the husband is the head of the wife just as Christ is the head of the church" (Eph. 5:22-23; see Col. 3:18). In light of the order of creation, how can women, who are created to be in subjection to men, possibly hold a position of leadership in the church where they would inevitably exercise authority over men?

Then two specific biblical texts appear to prohibit women not only from preaching but also from any active participation in public worship:

> Women should be silent in the churches. For they are not permitted to speak, but should be subordinate, as the law also says *(1 Cor. 14:34)*.

> Let a woman learn in silence with full submission. I permit no woman to teach or to have authority over a man; she is to keep silent. For Adam was formed first, then Eve; and Adam was not deceived, but the woman was deceived and became a transgressor. Yet she will be saved through childbearing, provided they continue in faith and love and holiness, with modesty *(1 Tim. 2:11-15)*.

Roman Catholics, Eastern Orthodox, and traditional Protestants further argue that the Bible consistently portrays God as male (we do not pray, "Our Mother in heaven"!). Likewise, God's only begotten Son became incarnate as a male human being. Episcopal theologian J. I. Packer states the matter of Jesus' gender as follows: "The New Testament presents him as the second man, the last Adam, our prophet, priest, and king (not prophetess, priestess, and queen), and he is all this precisely in his maleness. . . . That one male is best represented by another male is a matter of common sense; that Jesus' maleness is basic to his role as our incarnate Savior is a matter of biblical revelation."[15]

Biblical teaching seems crystal clear. Women are not permitted to speak (hence, teach or preach) in the church, nor are they permitted to exercise leadership roles over men. The issue appears to be quite simple: either we obey the clear teaching of Scripture or we disobey.

Is it, however, really that simple? Paul writes, just as unambiguously, for example: "Slaves, in all things obey those who are your masters . . . Masters, grant to your slaves justice and fairness" (Col. 3:22; 4:1, NASB). These scriptures have been used by generations of Christians to justify what John Wesley called "that most vile of sinful institutions." George Whitefield, Wesley's coevangelist during the early years of the great evangelical revival in England, responded to the slavery issue different from Wesley. He became the catalyst for the Great Awakening in the American colonies during the mid-1700s. His preaching drew crowds of thousands and precipitated one of the most astonishing revival movements in the history of our country. He castigated worldly living and pressed hard for moral reform. Yet when it came to slavery, he not only wrote tracts defending it as a biblically sanctioned institution but acquired a slave plantation in the mid-1740s with eight slaves. His only concerns were that masters would treat their "servants" well and work for their evangelization.[16]

At the height of the abolitionist movement to free slaves, Presbyterian theologian Robert Lewis Dabney advocated this strategy of opposing them in 1851: "Here is our policy then, to push the Bible argument continually, to drive Abolitionism to the wall, to compel it to assume an anti-Christian position."[17] The "Bible argument" pressed and upheld by the overwhelming majority of Southern ministers—and many Northern as well—was: first, slavery was an accepted institution in both Testaments; second, neither prophet nor priest, neither Jesus nor Paul ever uttered one word specifically condemning it; and third, slavery is a social institution ordained of God as part of the created hierarchy by which human relationships are ordered. Baptist theologian Dr. Richard Furman argued from the silence of the Bible to speak out against slavery in this manner: "Had the holding of slaves been a moral evil, it cannot be supposed that the inspired Apostles, who feared not the faces of men, and were ready to lay down their lives for the cause of their God, would have tolerated it, for a moment, in the Christian Church. . . . In proving this subject justifiable by Scriptural authority, its morality is also proved; for the Divine Law never sanctions immoral actions."[18]

Many defenders of slavery saw in it the providential hand of God in that "heathenish pagans" were delivered from a burning hell because of their good fortune to be brought to a country where they could be under the influence of the gospel. The fact that so many slaves did embrace Christianity only reinforced their belief. Furthermore, Christianity had the added advantage of pacifying the slaves and making them better workers. A young black fugitive named Frederick Douglass, addressing a white audience in Boston during January 1842, gave them a sampling of the kind of preaching slaves typically heard as they sat segregated in a balcony. White Southern clergymen would take a biblical text such as "Do to others as you would have them do to you" (Luke 6:31), and this is the way they would apply it:

> They would explain it to mean, "slaveholders, do unto *slaveholders* what you would have them do unto you":—and then looking impudently up to the slaves' gallery . . . looking high up to the poor colored drivers and the rest, and spreading his hands gracefully

abroad, he says, (mimicking,), "And you too, my friends, have souls of infinite value—souls that will live through endless happiness or misery in eternity. Oh, *labor diligently* to make your calling and election sure. Oh, receive into your souls these words of the holy apostle—'Servants, be obedient unto your masters.' Oh, consider the wonderful goodness of God! Look at your hard, horny hands, your strong muscular frames, and see how mercifully he has adapted you to the duties you are to fulfil! While to your masters, who have slender frames and long delicate fingers, he has given brilliant intellects, that they may do the *thinking*, while you do the *working*."[19]

The slavery issue was no academic matter. Ultimately, it was settled, not in church councils nor by legislative action, but on the battlefield. A total of 529,332 Americans laid down their lives during the Civil War, nearly as many as have died in all other American wars combined.

Another shocking example of the damage done through faulty biblical interpretation can be cited. In 1828, some white members of a Dutch Reformed congregation in South Africa refused to partake of the Lord's Supper with the "colored" husband of a Malay slave. They argued, on the basis of 1 Cor. 8:13, that if the presence of a colored person at Holy Communion offended some whites, the dark-skinned one should stay away so as not to "offend" (KJV). This was the inauspicious beginning of what has become one of the most heinous, discriminatory, and incendiary social systems in the world today, apartheid. Supporters of "apartness" interpret the Tower of Babel story to mean that God himself ordained the separation of the races. Proponents of biblical separation of the races also cite the differing languages given to the disciples on the Day of Pentecost as evidence of divine approval for maintaining strict ethnic homogeneity and separation.[20] Already the struggle over apartheid has claimed the lives of tens of thousands and deprived millions of others of "freedom, liberty and justice for all."

We could add to the list other questionable practices that are defended as "biblical": polygamy, dancing, consumption of alcoholic beverages, snake handling, works salvation, free love, and divorce. A biblical case can be made for child sacrifice, for the burning of witches, for stoning people who gather sticks on the Sabbath, for abandoning spouses and children, and even for genocide. Likewise, biblical support can be found for nearly every position under the sun relative to male-female roles in church and home.

It is important, at the outset, to establish an overall framework for biblical interpretation. It is quite clear that earnest, Spirit-filled, Bible-believing Christians can have strong differences of opinion about the Scriptures. Furthermore, when virtually every strange belief and bizarre behavior imaginable can be buttressed by biblical texts, it is obvious that the Bible can be understood in almost as many ways as there are readers. How do we sort through this jungle of claims and counterclaims, so that we "no longer [are] children, tossed to and fro and blown about by every wind of doctrine, by people's trickery, by their craftiness in deceitful scheming" (Eph. 4:14)?

There are certain basic principles that guide us as we interpret the Scriptures in the evangelical, Wesleyan-Arminian tradition. Among biblical scholars, there is a truism that holds that "interpreting a text out of context is a pretext." Never is that "truism" more true than in analyzing what the Bible has to say about women, particularly when it comes to Paul's teachings—which appear, at first reading, to deny women equal standing with men in church and home.

First of all, we must see what the text actually says. Translation is by no means an exact science. One word in Hebrew or Greek may allow for a dozen or more English words to be used. Which option is exercised makes a lot of difference in how the English reader understands the text. We shall see this, particularly in the way such words as *head* and *subjection* are used. What these words mean in Greek and suggest in English are vastly different.

Second, we must take careful note of the immediate context of a scriptural passage. We believe that the Bible is the inspired ("God-breathed") Word of God. Yet not every word in the Bible is God's. "Holy men of God spake as they were moved by the Holy Ghost" (2 Pet. 1:21, KJV), but so did a number of unholy men and women, beginning with Adam and Eve. The Bible records the words not only of the wise but also of the foolish, not only of angels but also of demons, not only of "apostles and prophets" but also of sorcerers and Satan. By ignoring the immediate context, the Bible can be construed to teach atheism ("There is no God," Ps. 14:1) and to promote hedonism ("Let us eat and drink, for tomorrow we die," 1 Cor. 15:32). When we consider the context of Paul's admonition, "Women should be silent in the churches" (14:34), for instance, we will discover that he is endeavoring to restore some semblance of order in a very disorderly church, where certain women (*"the* women") were disrupting the worship services with their tongues-speaking, idle chatter, and interruptive questions. It was not a rule prohibiting all women from ever speaking in church.

Third, a particular passage must be evaluated in the larger context of all that a particular author has to say, as well as the intention and purpose of the Bible in its entirety. It does violence to the apostle Paul's high view of women, for instance, to focus exclusively on a few select passages where he is addressing problem situations and to ignore the larger portrait of all he has to say about women, particularly the equality they enjoy as full partners with men in all aspects of the life and ministry of the church.

Then each author must be interpreted in light of the big picture of all God is doing by way of creation, redemption, resurrection, and restoration, throughout the vast sweep of Scripture. John Wesley (1703-91), founder of Methodism and the spiritual and theological forefather of the holiness movement, encouraged us to judge every text according to "the general tenor of Scripture."[21] He further counseled that "every doubted scripture [must be] interpreted according to the grand truths which run through the whole."[22] That "grand truth" finds its locus, its apex, its full and final expression in "[Jesus] Christ himself, in whom are hidden all the treasures of wisdom and knowledge" (Col. 2:2c-3).

Wesley maintained, along with Martin Luther (1483-1546) and John Calvin (1509-64), that Christ is the "central point of the circle" around which everything in Scripture revolves.[23] Luther spoke of the Scriptures as the manger in which lies the Christ child. He often referred to Christ as the "King of Scripture." Everything in Scripture must be judged in light of Jesus, in whom "all the fulness of Deity dwells in bodily form" (Col. 2:9, NASB). This is known as the "Christological Principle" of biblical interpretation. For instance, we must ask: Was it Jesus' intention, in selecting only male apostles, to thereby exclude women from publicly proclaiming the gospel, or were there some practical social realities that dictated such a limitation? Can we find clear support in the life and teachings of Jesus for dividing the Body of Christ along gender lines? Was it His purpose for His "body" to institutionalize discrimination against women? Does this state of affairs in today's church bring Him glory?

In analyzing a particular passage, these questions must be asked: Who is speaking? To whom are the words addressed? Why? What is going on? What are the author's intentions? How was it read and understood by its first readers? How do we translate that from the biblical world to ours?

Fourth, we must distinguish between what is *descriptive* and what is *prescriptive* in the Bible. In telling the story of Cain who killed Abel in a fit of rage (Gen. 4:1-16), the Bible does not suggest that this represents how brothers ought to relate to one another. Rather, we are commanded, over and over again, to "love one another, because love is from God" (1 John 4:7). In light of this principle, we will ask: Does the curse, directed to Eve, *prescribe* how men and women are to relate to each other in perpetuity—even in Christ—or does it rather *describe* the consequences of the Fall?

Fifth, we need to recognize the difference between the *particular* and the *universal*, between what is historically conditioned and what is timeless truth. For instance, Jesus commanded His disciples to "go . . . to the lost sheep of the house of Israel" and forbade them from preaching to the Gentiles (Matt. 10:5-6). We can easily discern, however, that this command was in no way intended to be universal but represented a particular directive for a specific mission, in that Jesus later commissioned these same apostles to "go therefore and make disciples of all nations" (28:19; cf. Acts 1:8). Likewise, when Paul counseled Timothy to "drink . . . a little wine" (1 Tim. 5:23), we do not take that to mean all Christians are obliged to consume alcoholic beverages. We will argue that Paul's instruction to Timothy, prohibiting women from teaching or exercising authority over men (2:12), does not prescribe a universal law but describes how he dealt with a specific and unique problem situation that arose in a particular church, the church at Ephesus.

Sixth, we need to be fully aware of the historical, social, and cultural context that forms the background of a given scripture. We will be at a loss to understand why the disciples "marveled that [Jesus] had been speaking with a woman" (John 4:27, NASB) until we discover that, in New Testament times, Jewish men never spoke with women in public. It is only when we understand the social customs that severely restricted the public role of women in first-century Palestine that we can resolve the apparent contradiction between Paul's instruction for the women in Corinth to keep silent in the church (1 Cor. 14:34-35) and his teaching that "there is no longer male and female; for all of you are one in Christ Jesus" (Gal. 3:28). Our principal task, then, is to discover what is the "grand truth" of the whole of Scripture in regard to male-female relationships in general and then what is the role of women in the church in particular.

Finally, we must distinguish between God's *original intentions* for us and His *accommodation* to our fallen estate. For instance, nobody believes that God's command for Joshua to destroy all the peoples in the land of Canaan represents either His best will or His ultimate design in dealing with enemies (see Matt. 5:44; Luke 9:51-56). Likewise, Christians have held, from the New Testament era onward, that many of God's instructions to the Israelites regarding circumcision, sacrifices, feasts, and ritual laws did not represent a permanent order but rather a temporary and provisional expedient. In responding to the Pharisee's shabby question on "whether it was lawful for a man to divorce his wife" (Mark 10:2, NASB), Jesus answered by pointing out that Moses' divorce law was an accommodation to their "hardness of heart" (v. 5). God's original intention was that "a man shall leave his father and mother, and the two shall become one flesh" (v. 7, NASB). Jesus went so far as to add to the text of Gen. 2:24, "Therefore what God has joined together, let no one separate" (v. 9). He did so deliberately and with authority, confident that He was bearing witness to God's original purposes for marriage and the family. Our task, then, will be to separate that which is culturally derived from that which owes its genesis to the great purposes for humankind, revealed in creation and realized in Jesus.

We must acknowledge, at the outset, that the Scriptures were written in, and deeply reflective of, a patriarchal culture. It was, in biblical times, a "man's world." The principal actors, throughout the Bible, are males. The Old Testament does not speak of the God of "Sarah, Rachel, and Rebekah" but of "Abraham . . . , Isaac . . . , and Jacob" (Exod. 3:15). All the priests were men, as were Israel's judges—except for Deborah (Judg. 4:4). All the kings of Israel were men, as were the prophets—except for Huldah, who was a noteworthy prophetess during the reign of Josiah (2 Kings 22:14-20). Biblical writers do use male pronouns and images in speaking of God, though not exclusively, as we shall see. Jesus was incarnate as a male human being. John Paul II is only the most recent in a long line of Catholic popes and Protestant traditionalists who steadfastly defend barring women from the priesthood and ordained ministry by making the point that "Jesus chose 12 apostles and not one of them was a woman." Such an argument invites the response: Jesus chose 12 apostles and not one of them was a Gentile either!

We have every right to question, however, whether patriarchy represents God's original intention and ultimate design as to how men and women are to relate to each other. If we accept such a hierarchical model as reflective of God's immutable order, then we must admit that those who defended slavery as an extension of that same hierarchical order were justified.

And so, as biblical interpreters, we must constantly ask ourselves whether any given practice, commandment, or institution recorded in the Scriptures reflects God's patient, provisional, and gracious accommodation to fallen humankind's desperate situation under the curse of sin, or represents how things were meant to be by way of His original, creative intention and the redemption that is "in Christ." Then we have a choice to make: either to live according to the rule of the law or to live within the reign of grace where "there is no longer male and female; for all of you are one in Christ Jesus" (Gal. 3:28). "For the Law was given through Moses; grace and truth were realized through Jesus Christ" (John 1:17, NASB).

·2

Women in History: Less than Human

*W*hat is striking about the "Danvers Statement," which asserts patriarchal roles in church and home, is that it is not striking at all. It represents, rather, a reaffirmation of the principle of male dominance and female subordination that has characterized virtually all human societies since the dawn of recorded history.

Women have constituted the most discriminated-against majority in every civilization, culture, race, nation, and religion. They have been relegated to a second-class status and treated as a subhuman species. They have been denied citizenship, education, civil or legal rights, and a voice or a vote in any public assembly. For instance, women did not gain the right to vote in England until 1919 and in the United States until 1920. They have been treated as property to be bought, sold, or cast aside when they no longer served men's purposes. "Woman has been treated as man's inferior so long," protests Patricia Gundry, "that this practice has become accepted as truth."[1]

There have been rare and isolated exceptions to this devaluation of women. In Egypt, Greece, and the later Roman empire, there were periods of time in which some women attained a high degree of emancipation. Some Greek women in Sparta attained an education and took part in public life. Many Roman women achieved a high degree of wealth and influence, although none ever became Caesar or were elected to the senate. But even in these relatively brief periods of history, it was generally only the well-born and highly positioned women who were able to break the bonds of inferiority and subordination. Even as water seeks its own level, these brief episodes of women asserting themselves faded back into the servility of social patriarchalism.

In order for us to develop some sense of appreciation for the radicalness of the New Testament's noble vision of women's emancipation, it is vitally important to gain some comprehension of how women have been regarded and treated.

WOMEN IN PRIMITIVE SOCIETIES

An extreme but not atypical example of the oppression and brutalization of women in primitive cultures is reported by Robert Hughes in his definitive history of Australia. He cites an earlier account by George Barrington (1802), which describes aboriginal courtship as follows:

> In obtaining a female partner the first step they take, romantic as it may seem, is to fix on some female of a tribe at enmity with their own. . . . The monster then stupefies her with blows, which he inflicts with his club, on her head, back, neck, and indeed every part of her body, then snatching up one of her arms, he drags her, streaming with blood from her wounds, through the woods, over stones, rocks, hills and logs, with all the violence and determination of a savage, till he reaches his tribe.[2]

As overdrawn as this portrait might seem, courtship by violence and rape was not uncommon. Aboriginal women had no rights at all and could choose nothing. A girl was generally given away when she was born. She was the absolute property of her kin until marriage and then the virtual slave of her husband after that. She was merely a "root-grubbing, shell-gathering chattel, whose social assets were wiry arms, prehensile toes and a vagina."[3] Aborigines were nomadic wanderers. On the march it was up to each woman to carry her infants as well as food and implements. Since she could carry only one child, the others would either be left to starve or be beaten to death. Wives were lent to visitors and swapped as a sign of brotherhood. They were sent out to test the intentions of a potentially threatening aggressor. If peaceful, the intruders would have relations with them. If the women returned untouched, that was regarded as an insult that had to be answered in battle. An exchange of wives capped a truce between enemies. If a woman showed the least reluctance to be used for these purposes, or seemed lazy, or otherwise offended her lord and master, she would be "furiously beaten or even speared."[4]

Another example comes from the journal of Samuel Hearne, the first European explorer to venture far north into the Canadian arctic in the mid-1700s. He and his party would have perished of starvation had they not been rescued by a native Indian chief by the name of Matonabee. Farley Mowat quotes Hearne's journal in which a typically demeaning view of women is graphically expressed:

> Matonabee attributed our present misfortunes partly to the misconduct of our guides, but mainly to the insistence of the Governor that we should take no women.
>
> "For," said he, "when all the men are heavy laden, they can neither hunt nor travel any distance. And in case they should meet with some success in hunting, who is to carry the produce of their labour? Women were made for labour. One of them can carry or haul as much as two men. They also pitch our tents, make and mend our clothes, keep us warm at night—and in

fact there is no such thing as travelling any consider-
able distance without their assistance. More than this,
women can be maintained at trifling expense, for, as
they always cook, the very licking of their fingers in
scarce times is sufficient for their sustenance."[5]

Even though Africa has been heavily influenced by
Western culture, traditional attitudes toward women persist among most tribes. Women are virtual slaves. They not
only carry the full responsibility for domestic duties but also do all the work toward maintaining their home and
family. They plow, plant, till, and harvest the crops. When
missionaries, as recently as the turn of the 20th century,
suggested that farmers could increase the yield of their
fields by utilizing oxen to pull their plows, the tribesmen
protested that cattle should not be used to do women's
work. Women draw and carry the water. They gather, cut,
and haul the firewood with no help from their husbands.
A traveler to Africa is immediately struck by the anomaly
of women carrying immense loads on their heads or on
their backs supported by a strap over their foreheads,
while men are rarely seen carrying anything. Furthermore,
men and women never hold hands in public, or otherwise
display any sign of affection. Rarely does one see a man
carrying on a conversation with a woman, least of all his
wife.

Husbands are the undisputed monarchs of their
households. A man can have as many wives as he can afford while the woman has no choice in the matter. Among
some tribes husbands do not sleep with their wives except
for purposes of procreation. They do not eat with their
wives and children. When the wife brings him his food,
she places it on the ground before him so that he will not
be contaminated by her touch. He then pulls it toward
himself with his foot. Wives and children may be beaten,
burnt, stabbed, and even slain by their husbands and fa-

thers at their will and whim. If a woman's husband dies, she becomes the property of the husband's family. Any male family member may have her. Children born of these unions will carry the name of her deceased husband.

WOMEN IN GREECE AND ROME

Greek philosophers not only bequeathed to the world the settled conviction that women were inferior to men but taught that it was an indisputable fact of natural law. Around this prejudice they wove such a tight web of reason that it became an unquestioned assumption throughout the subsequent course of Western history—at least until the 19th century. It is ironic that such an unflattering view of women would originate in Athens, the city named after Athenia, the lovely goddess of wisdom.

Pythagoras (ca. 580-ca. 500 B.C.), one of the earliest Greek philosophers, wrote, "There is a good principle which created order, light and man, and an evil principle which created chaos, darkness and woman." Socrates (ca. 470-399 B.C.) described women as "the weaker sex" and taught that they were halfway between a man and an animal. He asked, "Do you know anything at all practiced among mankind, in which in all these respects the male sex is not far better than the female?"[6]

Plato (ca. 428-347 B.C.), who recorded and immortalized the teachings of Socrates, was embraced by the Church fathers because his philosophical framework was so compatible with many features of Christian theology. It was inevitable, then, that Socrates' low opinion of women would be accepted as authoritative. Plato's influential disciple, Aristotle (384-322 B.C.), wrote that all females, both animal and human, were inferior to males: "While still within the mother the female takes longer to develop than the male does . . . because females are weaker and colder in their nature; and we should look upon the female state as being as it were a deformity, though one which occurs in the ordinary course of nature."[7]

Aristotle further taught that men are made for commanding and women for obeying and that this inequality is permanent. The difference between man and woman is like that of soul and body: the man is to his wife like a soul is to a body, commanding and guiding its members with intelligence and wisdom. Aristotle used the same analogy to define the relationship between master and slave. He warned that the "equality of the two or rule of the inferior is always hurtful."[8] This sentiment still reverberates in the 20th century. Marabel Morgan writes, in her popular "submissionism" text *The Total Woman*, that "it is only when a woman surrenders her life to her husband, reveres and worships him, and is willing to serve him, that she becomes really beautiful to him."[9] A Texas state senator was recently quoted in a newspaper, echoing the philosophers' view of women when he asked, "Do you know why God created women? Because sheep can't type."

Respectable Greek wives lived secluded in their homes. They were denied a voice or vote in any public affairs and were forbidden to either eat or socialize with men. Women were excluded from the marketplace, sporting events, and the agora where philosophy was discussed. Women were married at an early age to men they did not know. They received no education apart from learning domestic duties. The ideal woman, according to Xenophon, a contemporary of Aristotle, was one who "might see as little as possible, hear as little as possible, and ask as little as possible."[10] A friend of Xenophon described his wife in these terms: "She was not yet fifteen when I introduced her to my house, and she had been brought up always under the strictest supervision; as far as could be managed, she had not been allowed to see anything, hear anything or ask any questions."[11] Pericles stated

that it was the duty of an Athenian mother to live so retired a life that her name would never be mentioned
among men, either for praise or for shame.[12]

WOMEN IN PALESTINE

Nowhere do we witness the dehumanizing and demeaning effects of religious and social patriarchalism more
clearly than in the Judaism of Jesus' day. New Testament
scholars, such as Joachim Jeremias, have been able to reconstruct a detailed portrait of how women were viewed
and treated.[13]

Women were to be secluded from public life. They
were to remain in the inner chamber of the house and de-
vote themselves solely to domestic duties. When they went
out in public their heads were covered and their faces
veiled so that their features could not be recognized. Only
on the day of her wedding was a bride seen with head uncovered, and then only if she were a virgin. For a woman
to appear in public with her face uncovered was sufficient
cause for her husband to divorce her. Rabbinical literature
expresses high regard for those women who kept their
head covered even in their own house, so that their children would grow to maturity without ever seeing their
mother's face. On one occasion a chief priest in Jerusalem
failed to recognize that the woman before him, charged
with adultery, was his own mother. It is difficult to imagine
any social custom more depersonalizing and dehumanizing to women than covering up their faces. Men did not
treat their animals like that!

When a woman ventured out, the Mishnah (Traditions
of the Elders) forbade a man to give her a greeting or even
to look at her. It was disgraceful for a rabbi to speak with a
woman in public. It was preferable for a woman, especially
unmarried, to avoid going out at all. "I was a pure maiden
and I strayed not from my father's house," boasted the

mother of seven sons martyred during the wars of Jewish independence (ca. 150 B.C.). The Talmud interprets the words of Ps. 45:13, "The king's daughter is all glorious within" (KJV), as a description of the secluded life of women who never leave their houses. There are numerous accounts in Jewish literature about women, such as Salome who danced before Herod's guests, flouting dress codes, but they are always viewed with extreme disfavor as representing "loose women." There was one exception to this rule: twice a year dances took place in the vineyards around Jerusalem when unmarried maidens, whose fathers had been unable to arrange a marriage, were allowed to parade their facial beauty before eligible Jewish males. There is evidence that headdress codes were not as strictly observed in the country as in the town, yet even there it was not proper for a man to talk with a woman.

A Jewish woman had the legal status of a slave and was regarded as a possession of her father and then of her husband. She had no legal rights of her own. This was based on a rabbinical interpretation of the 10th commandment, which reads: "You shall not covet your neighbor's house; you shall not covet your neighbor's wife or his male servant or his female servant or his ox or his donkey or anything that belongs to your neighbor" (Exod. 20:17, NASB). A woman thus had the same status as a house, slave, ox, and donkey. She was denied any education other than learning domestic arts. She could not receive an inheritance nor keep any money she earned. A father could sell his daughter into slavery until she was 12. Daughters were valued primarily as a source of profit and cheap labor. Her father, or her husband, represented her in all legal matters, in which she had no voice whatsoever. He could cancel any vows that she made.

A father arranged for his daughter's marriage, generally shortly after she was born. He retained the dowry, which her fiancé had to pay. Up until the age of 12 she had no right to refuse such a marriage. He could marry her even to someone with a crippling deformity. The Mishnah provided that a wife could be acquired "by money, or by writ, or by intercourse." Marriage contracts were drawn up with wives considered as the acquisition of their husbands, just as if they were Gentile slaves. Marriages among relatives were preferred. For a man to marry his sister's daughter, his own niece, is praised in Jewish literature as a pious act. There are frequent accounts of intrafamily marriages, like that of Abraham to his half-sister Sarah, and Jacob to his cousins, Leah and Rachel. While a woman could have only one husband, a man could have as many wives as he could afford. Upon marriage, ownership of the woman passed from her father to her husband. Her sole reason for existence was to bear him children and to meet his every need. Failure to bear children was a great misfortune and was even considered a divine punishment (cf. Luke 1:25). Her only hope of gaining any respect whatsoever was to bear her husband a son. If her husband died without leaving her with a son, she was still bound by Moses' Levirate law of marriage to her husband's brothers until they either raised up a son by her to carry on her deceased husband's name and inheritance, or until they published a refusal to do so. Without this she could not remarry (Deut. 25:5-10; cf. Mark 12:18-27).

A wife's role was strictly domestic. Her duties were to spin, weave, sew, and wash clothes for her husband. She was also responsible for grinding meal, baking, cooking, preparing and serving his meals. She was not permitted to eat with him but was to remain standing behind him while he ate. Other duties included clothing him, washing his face, hands, and feet, preparing his bed, and caring for him when he grew old. She had to turn over to him all money earned from manual work. She rendered to her husband unquestioning and absolute obedience in all things. This was a religious duty. Children were commanded to put respect for their father before that of their mother. If the family's life was in danger, the husband was to be saved first, sons second, then mother and daughters.

A husband could take another wife or concubine without consulting his first wife, and she was expected not only to welcome them into her home but also to live in harmony with them. Only the husband had the right of divorce. Moses permitted divorce if the husband found "some indecency in her" (Deut. 24:1, NASB). There were two schools of interpretation over the meaning of Moses' divorce law. The school of Shammai held that "some indecency" meant unchastity. The followers of Hillel, however, maintained that a husband was justified in turning his wife out of house and home for any reason of displeasure, even if he chanced to find more pleasure in another woman! The only stipulation was that he had to give her the sum of money prescribed in the marriage contract, which served as a form of alimony and child support. If she violated any number of rules, however, such as allowing a man to speak to her in public, she would forfeit the money. In practice, a divorced woman rarely was paid anything.

Women were denied any active role in religious life. With only a few exceptions, they were bound under all the prohibitions of the Law and were subject to the full force of the Law including the death penalty. They were not bound, however, to fulfill many of the positive commandments of the Law. For instance, they were under no obligation to make a pilgrimage to Jerusalem, to celebrate the three major festivals of the year, or to recite the daily Shema (Deut. 6:4-9). Girls were barred from attending rabbinical schools lest they learn how to read and thus gain access to the Law. Rabbi Eliezer (ca. A.D. 90) warned, "If a man gives his daughter a knowledge of the Law it is as though he taught her lechery." The reasoning behind this was that if a young woman should become conversant in the Law, she would want to discuss it with men. In so exposing herself, they would be more likely to become enticed into immorality.

Women could not offer sacrifices. They were forbidden to go into the inner courts of the Temple. They were not permitted to be in any part of the Temple precincts—even the Court of the Gentiles—while menstruating, nor for a period of 40 days after the birth of a son and 80 days after the birth of a daughter. Women were barred from participating in synagogue worship. The synagogue service was divided into two parts. Women could attend the *sabbateon*, devoted to the liturgy of worship, as long as they sat in a balcony or behind a latticework at the back of the sanctuary, thereby remaining hidden from the view of the worshiping men. They could not enter the synagogue by the front door but only by the back. They were not permitted to participate in singing, prayers, or responses in deference to "the dignity of the congregation." They had to maintain absolute silence. They were dismissed before the second part of the service called the *andron* (male), the "men's service," which was devoted to reading and expounding the Torah by the scribes. The rationale for excluding women was based upon the belief that since Eve was deceived, and thus was responsible for bringing sin into the world, all her daughters were thereby bound under a curse that rendered them unworthy to hear—much less to discuss or to teach—the Law of God. One rabbi said that "it would be better that the Torah be burnt than spoken from the lips of a woman." Philo, a contemporary of Jesus and Paul, taught that had there been no Eve, Adam would have remained happy and immortal. This practice of excluding women continues in force to the present day in Orthodox Jewish synagogues.

Women were forbidden to pray aloud over a meal at their own table. Even today women are barred from praying at the Wailing Wall in Jerusalem and can only look down upon the men at prayer from an observation area on top of the wall. Also, Jewish mothers are still barred from participating in their own sons' bar mitzvah.

Women had no civil rights, nor could they serve as witnesses in legal proceedings. Women were regularly described as being in the same class with Gentile slaves and minor children. Jewish literature is full of expressions of joy over the birth of a son and sorrow over the birth of a daughter. Two hundred years before Christ, Jesus ben Sirach lamented the excessive burdens a father had to bear over his daughter. He concluded, "Better is the wickedness of a man than a woman who does good; and it is a woman who brings shame and disgrace." A rabbinic verse-by-verse commentary on Genesis describes women as "greedy, eavesdroppers, lazy, and jealous . . . also querulous and garrulous." Rabbi Hillel taught that wherever many women were gathered together, there was much witchcraft. The Shabbath, which dates from around the time of Christ, describes woman as being "a pitcher full of filth with its mouth full of blood." Rabbi Judah encouraged Jewish males to utter three thanksgivings daily: "Blessed be He who did not make me a Gentile . . . a woman . . . a boor [ignorant of the law]." Another version of that popular prayer went, "Blessed be He who did not make me a Gentile, a dog, a woman"—in that order. The Gospel of Thomas, a second-century Gnostic letter widely circulated among the churches, contains supposedly "secret teachings" of Jesus. It concludes with this dialogue:

Simon Peter said to them, "Let Mary leave us, because women are not worthy of life."

Jesus said, "Behold, I shall guide her so as to make her male, that she too may become a living spirit like you men. For every woman who makes herself male will enter the kingdom of heaven."[14]

It is in light of this cultural and social background, dominant not only in Palestine but throughout the Mediterranean world, that the New Testament must be read. We will discover that neither Jesus nor Paul ever reflected such a low estimate of women. To the contrary, the New Testament explodes upon its world as one of the most egalitarian documents in history in the way it smashes walls and bridges chasms that have divided people from each other, all across the religious, racial, social, and gender spectrum. The gospel of Jesus Christ elevates women as coequal with men in all matters pertaining to the kingdom of God and to their life together as fellow members of the Body of Christ. The New Testament presents us with the earliest and most compelling vision of what a community of believers can become when "there is no longer Jew or Greek, there is no longer slave or free, there is no longer male and female; for all of you are one in Christ Jesus" (Gal. 3:28).

WOMEN IN CHURCH HISTORY

The emancipation and elevation of women that began in the ministry of Jesus and flowered in the earliest Church was, unfortunately, soon compromised and then finally lost. The rapidly growing and expanding Church, flooded by recent converts from Judaism and paganism, began to revert to the prevailing cultural estimate of women's inferiority until, by the middle of the second century A.D., Tertullian, the influential Church father and theologian, spelled out this rule as one of the precepts of ecclesiastical discipline concerning women: "It is not permitted for a woman to speak in the church, nor is it permitted for her to teach, nor to baptize, nor to offer [the eucharist], nor to claim for herself a share in any *masculine* function—not to mention any priestly office."[15]

There were a number of seemingly justifiable reasons for this retrenchment. First, the Church was primarily concerned with carrying out the Great Commission and establishing the Church in an alien and often hostile environment. It is too much to expect that it would immediately challenge unjust social institutions and undertake massive social reform, given how tiny, fragile, and vulnerable it was in its earliest decades. It was in a continuous fight for its very survival against heretics from within and harassment from without. There was scandal enough in the proclamation of the Cross without pressing for social reform. It was easier, and necessary, to conform to accepted social customs and cultural traditions rather than challenge them. It was revolutionary enough that they welcomed slaves and women into their fellowship at all.

More determinative in the Church's retrenchment back into patriarchalism was the rise and rapid spread of gnosticism, the first all-out assault upon the integrity of the gospel of Jesus Christ, particularly in the second and third centuries. As we shall see, the precursors of this insidious heresy can be found in the church at Ephesus while Timothy was its pastor. One of the seductive aspects of gnosticism, especially attractive to women, was its insertion of the female principle into both God and Christ. It represented an accommodation of Christianity to various features of goddess religions, and their veneration of the divine Mother as the complement [and sometimes consort] of the Father God. Many Gnostics regarded the Holy Spirit as female in gender—and with some justification in that the Hebrew word for Spirit is in the feminine case. In the Gnostic gospel the Apocryphon of John, the beloved apostle reports a vision in which God says, "I am the one who [is with you] always. I [am the Father]; I am the Mother; I am the Son."[16] The Gospel to the Hebrews has Jesus speaking of "my Mother, the Spirit."[17]

Many of the Gnostic writings portray women as recipients of "special revelation" from the risen Christ. Thus they became authoritative voices within some Christian communities, bearing "secret knowledge" that enabled the spirit to escape the imprisonment of body and soul until it ascended into the presence of absolute light, God. Women not only are prominently featured in Gnostic literature but were active in its propagation among the churches. One of the most influential Gnostic preachers, during the second century, was Marcion. He was a radical Christian who rejected the Hebrew Scriptures along with its repressive laws. He appointed women as priests and bishops and relied heavily upon them to spread his brand of Christian theology. Among the Valentinians, another Gnostic sect, women were encouraged to preach, teach, travel as evangelists and healers, and also functioned as priests. This prompted Tertullian to express his outrage: "These heretical women—how audacious they are! They have no modesty; they are bold enough to teach, to engage in argument, to enact exorcisms, to undertake cures, and, it may be, even to baptize!"[18]

The Montanists were another second-century radical movement. Though not Gnostic, they rejected the orthodox church with its priests as being corrupt and worldly. They relied upon direct messages from God rather than the Scriptures and believed that Montanus and two of their prophetesses, Priscilla and Maximilla, were mouthpieces for the Holy Spirit.

In their efforts to combat false doctrine and rid themselves of these heretical movements, the Church fathers reacted against not only their doctrines but their propagators as well, which were, in the main, women. By denying women access to platforms from which they could disseminate their pernicious heresies, they hoped to deprive gnosticism of its voice and thus choke it out altogether.

Clement, bishop of Rome, wrote a letter to the still unruly church in Corinth early in the second century in which he counseled that women were to "remain in the rule of subjection."[19] While men and women sat together in the earliest church for worship, the orthodox catholic congregations began to segregate them once again, as in Jewish synagogues. By the end of the second century, active participation of women in worship was expressly condemned. Christian communities that defied this ban were branded as heretical. While strains of Gnostic teaching persisted in various segments of the Church for many centuries, women were barred from assuming any prophetic, priestly, or episcopal roles in Catholic—and later Orthodox—churches from A.D. 200 to the present.

By the second century A.D. Paul's letters were widely circulated among the churches and carried the authoritative weight of Scripture even though they were not formally declared so until Bishop Athanasius' 39th Festal Letter in A.D. 367, at which time our present canon of sacred Scriptures was established and sealed. The Church fathers frequently appealed to those passages in his letters where Paul restricts the active participation of women in the church. And so it has continued, down across the centuries, right into our own day. It wasn't until the Second Great Awakening and the rise of the American holiness movement in the last century that any serious and sustained challenge to gender discrimination against women was launched (see chap. 7).

We must note another factor that played a key role in the historic subjugation of women: namely, spiritually-minded men have long viewed women as carnal and seductive, the flesh-and-blood incarnation of temptation to evil, and thus archenemies of the soul. This attitude of horror and contempt for women by many Christian men, especially ascetics devoted to a life of separation and contemplation, was given gross expression by the French monk Roger de Caen in *Carmen de Mundi Contimptu:* "If her bowels and flesh were cut open, you would see what filth is covered by her white skin. If a fine crimson cloth covered a pile of foul dung, would anyone be foolish enough to love the dung because of it? . . . There is no plague which monks should dread more than woman; the soul's death."[20]

Thomas Aquinas, the 13-century Church theologian whose *Summa Theologia* became the textbook of Roman Catholic doctrine and teaching, had this to say about women:

> As regards the individual nature, woman is defective and misbegotten, for the active power in the male seed tends to the production of a perfect likeness according to the masculine sex; while the production of woman comes from defect in the active power, or from some material indisposition, or even from some external influence, such as that of a south wind, which is moist . . .

> Subjection is twofold. One is servile, by virtue of which a superior makes use of a subject for his own benefit; and this kind of subjection began after sin. There is another kind of subjection, which is called economic or civil, whereby the superior makes use of his subjects for their own benefit and good; and this kind of subjection existed even before sin. For the good of order would have been wanting in the human family if some were not governed by others wiser than themselves. So by such a kind of subjection woman is naturally subject to man, because in man the discernment of reason predominates.[21]

Martin Luther's courageous stand on the authority of the Word, over against the excesses of the Roman church, brought release from bondage to religious superstition and precipitated the Protestant reformation. Yet, unfortunately, his democratizing doctrine of the "priesthood of every believer" did not extend to women. He regarded them as unfit for preaching, ministering the sacraments, or holding any positions of leadership in the congregation, a position still maintained by Missouri Synod Lutheran churches today. Luther's offhand comment reflects his low estimate of women: "Girls begin to talk and to stand on their feet sooner than boys because weeds always grow up more quickly than good crops."

The Church not only has historically embraced patriarchalism with its low regard for women but has actively enforced it in the rare instances where a local culture was oriented otherwise. Annie Machisale-Muscopole is an active lay member of the Church of Central Africa-Presbyterian. She has traveled widely in Europe, Africa, and the United States speaking on women's issues. The Chewa culture of her native Malawi is one of the few where women were, for centuries, accorded high respect. They were regarded as the source of life because both male and female children come into the world through them. "The art of creating and sustaining life," she reports, "is understood to be a secret between God and women. Women are considered to be co-creators with God."[22] The Chewa culture was matriarchal. Their social and religious history is peopled by numerous heroic female prophetesses, priests, and rulers.

With the advent of the white missionaries, however, accompanied by militaristic colonialists in the 18th century, there came a radical destruction of Chewa religion, of much of their culture, and of their social relationships. These African women who had historically enjoyed respect and equal status with men became enslaved in their own country. They were taught to submit unquestioningly to their husbands, who in turn submitted to the white man whose greater intelligence was a sign that he was nearer to

God. Under the umbrella of civilization, many Malawi were captured by Arabs and sold as slaves to European and American merchants. When gold was discovered, the white men claimed African territory for the English crown.

Since gaining their independence, Malawi women have regained much of their former respect and status in society, tribal leadership, and education—everywhere except in their churches. Even though their parent Scottish Presbyterian church now permits the ordination of women, the African branch does not. It is still trapped in the colonial caste system. Nevertheless, Annie Muscopole points out that women are the backbone of the church. They hold the revival meetings, convert people and form them in the faith, teach Sunday School and adult education classes, visit the sick, and carry out other charitable acts. She relates a proverb of her people that describes their situation, "The hen knows when it is daylight, but it leaves it to the cock to make the announcement."[23]

Our generation can scarcely comprehend that one of the most basic of human rights, the opportunity to seek a college or university education, is a freedom only recently granted to women. The first institution of higher education in the United States—or in history for that matter—to accept female students was Oberlin College in Ohio, and that not until the 1830s. Hillsboro College is proud of its record as the first in Michigan to open its doors to women, yet that wasn't until 1865. Both were distinctly Christian colleges founded as a consequence of the great spiritual awakenings of the mid-1800s. Such historic and prestigious universities as Harvard and Yale did not follow suit until around the turn of the 20th century. The University of North Carolina grudgingly opened its doors to women only after they gained the right to vote in 1920. They had to agree, however, to abide by certain rules: they must "(a) be accompanied to a class by a chaperon; (b) sit in a group in the rear of the room; (c) wear gloves and hats; (d) remain in their seats till the men had left; and (e) not participate in the graduation ceremonies nor have their picture in the yearbook."[24]

This is only the briefest sketch of what Elise Boulding calls, in the title of her book on women, *The Underside of History*.[25] In this pioneering work, she tries to tell the other half of *his*tory: namely, *her*story. It was a formidable task given the fact that the history of humankind has always been written by men as if it were the history of men. She has been able, nevertheless, to document the fact that women have occasionally transcended their culturally defined limits, carved out a space for themselves, and made significant contributions to their world in virtually every arena. She points out that "women have never been simply a subjugated people. They have always participated in a secondary way in the prevailing dominance structures of society."[26] Nevertheless, she concludes:

> Structures of dominance are ordinarily hierarchical. When the work of a number of people needs to be coordinated, hierarchical organization with successive levels of overview of the social scene eliminates a lot of explaining and teaching. If people do what they are told, "aboveness-belowness" works well. We have had ten thousand years of experience with progressive centralization of social organization. Few social scientists, let alone lay persons, could imagine doing without it.[27]

Even with "equal rights" consciousness so pervasive throughout the Western world today, it is difficult to imagine how things could work—in church, home, or society—apart from gender-powered social hierarchies. Most Christians cannot imagine anything different and thus defend the status quo as if it were God's first and final will for humankind. However, the question before those who have become new creatures in Christ Jesus, where the "old has passed away" and "everything has become new!" (2 Cor. 5:17), is this: Can we afford to continue our traditional patterns of being socially "conformed" to this present fallen world? Or is there a fresh wind of the Holy Spirit seeking to "transform" us by the renewing of our minds to "prove what the will of God is, that which is good and acceptable and perfect"? (Rom. 12:2, NASB). Can we, as children of God, continue to live as children of the world by denying to women full inclusion as coequal human beings with all the rights and privileges extended to men, simply because its has always been that way? Must we settle for the value systems of a fallen world under the shadow of sin's curse? Are we going to allow "this present age" to squeeze us into its narrow, restrictive, and prejudicial mold?

The Scriptures do reveal an alternative: a powerful, purifying, and exalted vision of how we can relate to each other in such a way that women are not de facto dehumanized and discriminated against but enjoy a status as coequal with men by virtue of the creative intention and the redemptive action of God in Christ. It is a truth that has been, for too long, denied. It is a story that must be told. To it we now turn.

3.

Women in the Old Testament

*T*he Bible gives us not only a vision of what ought to be but also a record of what, in fact, occurred. It is clear that most of biblical history reveals an unquestioned acceptance of a patriarchal social hierarchy in which women were under the dominion and rule of men. That, however, is neither the original ideal nor the only model of male-female relationships to be found in the Scriptures.

THE CREATION STORIES

All attempts to justify male dominance and female subordination biblically are grounded in the Genesis accounts of creation and fall. One of the foundational convictions of the "Danvers Statement," cited earlier, is that "Adam's headship in marriage was established by God before the Fall, and was not a result of sin." Elisabeth Elliot, missionary and author, writes, "I understand that women, by creation, have been given a place within the human level which is ancillary to that of men, and I am glad of this."[1] In their 1984 resolution excluding women from ordination and leadership in the church, the Southern Baptist Convention's rationale was "to preserve [the] submission God requires because man was first in creation and woman was first in the Edenic fall."[2] Augustine taught as much in *The*

Good of Marriage when he stated that the union of man and woman is "a kind of friendly and genuine union of one ruling and the other obeying."[3]

We must question, however, whether such a conclusion is justified. There are two separate and quite different accounts of creation in the first two chapters of Genesis, reflecting differing traditions. The first (Gen. 1:1—2:3) reads in part: "Then God said, 'Let us make humankind [adam] in our image, according to our likeness' . . . So God created humankind in his image, in the image of God he created them; male [zakar] and female [neqebah] he created them. God blessed them, and God said to them, 'Be fruitful and multiply, and fill the earth and subdue it; and have dominion over the fish of the sea and over the birds of the air and over every living thing that moves upon the earth'" (vv. 26-28).

Adam is a generic noun in Hebrew that means "human beings." Before differentiation according to gender, the man and the woman share an identical essence as "human beings." Male and female are created together, both having equal standing before God and between each other. The woman, like the man, is created in the image of God. Encompassed within God is that which corresponds not only to maleness but to femaleness as well. It is true that in speaking of God, biblical writers most often use masculine nouns and pronouns. Yet we ought no more to imagine that God is male than to assume He has a corporeal body because He is also described as having eyes, ears, arms, hands, legs, a back, and even wings. Such anthropomorphic descriptions of God reflect the limits of human comprehension and language and are to be regarded as metaphors. As one woman asked, "If God is a male and Jesus is a male, then where does that leave me?"

"God is spirit" (John 4:24) and thus beyond all gender classification.[4] Yet His image is equally represented in both male and female. Mary Hayter puts it this way: "It must be recognized that it is the 'Personhood,' not the 'sexuality,' of God which is the central point of the figure. . . . The God of Israel is more than any sexual appellation or image that may be used."[5] Male and female, then, are needed in order to fully reveal the nature of God and reflect His image. Aida Spencer further notes: "Even the New Testament writers are always careful to describe Jesus with the generic Greek term 'human' or *anthropos* rather than the term 'male' or *aner*. Although God became a male, God primarily became a human; otherwise, in some way males would be more saved than females. At creation, conversely, male and female form a unity. It is that unity which mirrors God's likeness."[6]

The woman receives the same blessing of God as the man: "God saw everything that he had made, and indeed, it was very good" (Gen. 1:31). Sinful man may demean, dehumanize, and despise woman, but God does not. She is by creation a choice and chosen human being and is by revelation as capable as the man in bearing and reflecting the image of God. Did the fall into sin so damage the relationship between male and female that the woman no longer reflects the image of God? Not according to the first genealogy recorded *after* the Fall: "This is the list of the descendants of Adam. When God created humankind, he made them in the likeness of God. Male and female he created them, and he blessed them and named them 'Humankind' when they were created" (5:1-2).

Again we see the parallel clauses, "he made him" and "he created them." Their name together was *Adam*, "human being." Neither their essential nature nor their ability to reflect God's image was changed. To both the command is given to "be fruitful and multiply." Both have equal responsibility in parenting, and to both is given the charge to exercise dominion over the earth. It is important to note

that, in the first creation account, there is no discussion—
not even a hint—of status or role differentiation between
the two.

There is, then, a full equality of personhood between
the man and the woman standing before God. Each is to
the other at once a horizon and a point of focus by which
they realize and rejoice in their own individuality. There is
not even a hint of hierarchical ordering between the sexes.
To the contrary, such arbitrary differentiation distorts their
spiritual nature as created in the image of God. Furthermore, it damages their ability to discover their own self-
identity. When the woman is devalued, the man's reflection of himself in her is thereby also diminished. When the
woman is restricted from achieving her full potential and
denied the exercise of her unique gifts, the image of God
reflected through her is truncated.

Those who appeal to a pre-Fall male-female hierarchy
do so, not on the basis of the first but the second creation
account, which reads in part:

> Then the Lord God formed man from the dust of
> the ground, and breathed into his nostrils the breath of
> life; and the man became a living being. . . . Then the
> Lord God said, "It is not good that the man should be
> alone; I will make him a helper as his partner." . . . So
> the Lord God caused a deep sleep to fall upon the
> man, and he slept; then he took one of his ribs and
> closed up its place with flesh. And the rib that the Lord
> God had taken from the man he made into a woman
> and brought her to the man. Then the man said, "This
> at last is bone of my bones and flesh of my flesh; this
> one shall be called Woman, for out of Man this one
> was taken." Therefore a man leaves his father and his
> mother and clings to his wife, and they become one
> flesh (2:7, 18, 21-24).

This passage suggests an "order of creation" by which
the hierarchical superiority of the man over the woman is

defended. Traditionalists, from Rabbinic Jews of pre-New Testament times to the framers of the "Danvers Statement," have concluded that since the woman came *after* the man and *from* the man, obviously she was inferior *to* the man. We must ask, however: Is this the clear teaching of the second creation account? Or is it an interpretation imposed upon it by patriarchal presuppositions? It is true that according to this passage the man was formed first and then the woman. However, if this implies male superiority, then it could be argued that since man came *after* the ground and *from* the dust, obviously he is inferior to dirt! If first in creation establishes a hierarchical ranking, then on the basis of the first creation account, we would have to conclude that fish, birds, and animals are superior to man.

The apostle Paul does acknowledge the unchallenged rabbinic assumption of his day, that male "headship" is based upon the belief that "man was not made from woman, but woman from man." However, he goes go on to say, **"Nevertheless,** in the Lord woman is not independent of man or man independent of woman. **For just as woman came from man, so man comes through woman;** but all things come from God" (1 Cor. 11:8, 11-12, emphasis added). In other words, after forming the original woman out of the first man, **God reversed the order:** from that time forward, all men are born of women! So much for the "order of creation"!

God was not bound by any wooden hierarchy in terms of His gracious election. He chose Jacob, the second-born, rather than Esau to become the ancestor of the Hebrew people. He chose Moses rather than his older brother, Aaron, to lead the children of Israel. He directed Samuel to choose David, the youngest rather than the oldest of Jesse's sons, to be king. Jesus demolished all social structures based upon artificially imposed hierarchies when He said,

"If anyone wants to be first, he shall be last of all, and servant of all" (Mark 9:35, NASB; see 10:43-44).

God formed man out of the dust of the earth. In order to show special kindness to the woman, however, God formed her out of the living flesh of the man. They are both "one flesh" (Gen. 2:24): not a superior flesh for the man and an inferior flesh for the woman. The woman was not created as a subordinate creature, a "help meet" as the KJV inaccurately translates it, but as a "helper like unto himself" or a "helper corresponding to himself" (see 2:18).[7] The Hebrew word *ezer*, "helper," refers to God in most instances where it is used in the Old Testament, who obviously is not in a subordinate position to the one He helps. Consequently, "helper" does not convey any implication of a gender-determined hierarchy whatsoever. When the Hebrew text was translated into Greek around 250 B.C., the Septuagint translators were careful to render "helper corresponding to himself" in such a way as to indicate a horizontal relationship rather than vertical hierarchy. Donald E. Gowan comments: "Indeed, this is the only creation story known from the ancient Near East that gives to woman such an important role. It has stood for centuries . . . as a radical challenge to the assumption of male supremacy. Jesus clearly heard it and acted upon it, and in our day we may rejoice in new efforts to understand its implication for life in family, church, and society."[8]

God's original intention for humankind, then, was that the man and the woman would together bear and reflect His own nature, would share with him as vice-regents governing the earth, while freely partaking of its bounty. Each would, in their intimate relationship and mutual partnership with each other, mirror the fellowship that He enjoys within himself as Father, Son, and Holy Spirit. The man could not fulfill the destiny for which he was created by himself. He needed someone "corresponding to himself." In work, marriage, and church, man and woman are to stand together, side by side, rendering mutual assistance to each another as together they actualize God's purposes and their own potential. In their spiritual development, they are to celebrate their unity as "one flesh" human beings by equally sharing in worship, leadership, and service. This is the exalted vision of the Hebrew prophets to whom was given the revelation of humankind as God intentioned it to be.

THE FALL

Though both Adam and Eve are implicated in the disobedience that brought sin and death into the world (Gen. 3:1-24), Eve has borne the brunt of the blame. Generations of Jews and Christians have unjustly assigned to the woman the greater responsibility for the Fall for these reasons. First, the woman was deceived and not the man. This has been interpreted to mean that women are the weaker sex and by nature more susceptible to sin than men. Second, since the woman was the first to eat of the forbidden fruit, she was the one who introduced sin into the world. After all, she did admit her culpability: "The serpent deceived me, and I ate" (v. 13, NASB). Third, she was the one who invited (seduced?) Adam to eat.

This provided more than enough biblical warrant for the Jewish males of Jesus' day to justify their debasing treatment of, and oppressive discrimination against, women. A century before Christ, Jesus ben Sirach wrote: "From a woman sin had its beginning, and because of her we all die" (Sirach 25:24).[9] This sentiment is echoed in a noncanonical Jewish writing, The Life of Adam and Eve 3, in which Eve is portrayed as saying to Adam: "My lord, if you want, kill me. Perchance the Lord God will then lead you back into Paradise, for it was only through my fault that the anger of the Lord God was kindled against you."[10]

Women were regarded as so corrupted—and corrupting—that a separatist Jewish sect fanatically devoted to holiness, the Qumran communities of Essenes who lived in isolated Dead Sea desert compounds around the time of Christ, forbade marriage or cohabitation. The men segregated themselves from the women. They shunned all contact with them lest they, too, be corrupted. Likewise, Tertullian based his disdain for women upon Eve's deception and sin: "God's sentence hangs still over all your sex and His punishment weighs down upon you. You are the devil's gateway; you are she who first violated the forbidden tree and broke the law of God. It was you who coaxed your way around him whom the devil had not the force to attack. With what ease you shattered that image of God; man! Because of the death you merited, the Son of God had to die."[11]

There is no question about the biblical fact that Eve was the first deceived, as Paul reminds Timothy (1 Tim. 2:14). However, does this justify holding that the "curse" directed specifically to Eve was intended to be perpetuated upon all of her female—and not male—descendants? Or are there other ways of reading the story of the Fall that deal more even-handedly with both Adam and Eve. Many scholars think so. It is important to note that the command not to eat from the tree of the knowledge of good and evil came to Adam and not to Eve, since she had not yet been created (Gen. 2:17). She only learned about it secondhand. It is likewise clear that both Adam and Eve were present throughout the dialogue with the serpent. The Hebrew text clearly shows that when the serpent speaks to the woman, the plural "you" is used rather than the feminine singular "you." The text also has the serpent saying, "For God knows that when you [plural] eat of it your [plural] eyes will be opened" (3:5).

Many have asked: Was Eve totally wrong in what she desired? One well-known undergraduate institution of higher learning wrote in a fund-raising letter: "Eve had the right idea. Surrounded in Eden by an infinitely varied, deliciously fascinating environment, she rejected the haven of blissful ignorance and reached for knowledge—of herself and the world around her."[12] The idea of a "happy fall" was embraced not only by the Gnostics but by some in the orthodox church tradition. A hymn survives from the sixth or seventh century that has this line, "O fortunate crime which merited to have such and so great a redeemer." The Roman Catholic missal represents the Fall as "fortunate" in that it necessitated the coming of Christ.[13]

It is obvious that there was much about the tree that was good and right: "The woman saw that the tree was good for food, and that it was a delight to the eyes, and that the tree was to be desired to make one wise" (Gen. 3:6). Surely there is nothing inherently wrong with food. Neither is it evil to appreciate that which is beautiful. Much less does the Bible discourage the quest for knowledge and understanding (e.g., the Book of Proverbs). According to Gen. 2:9, Eden was full of trees pleasant to the sight and good for food, from which Adam and Eve could freely eat. So there was nothing intrinsically evil in Eve's desire for nutrition, aesthetic enjoyment, and knowledge.

Eve's sin, and Adam's, was the underlying motivation behind eating of this particular fruit—to be as God, knowing good and evil (Gen. 3:5). Consuming the fruit became a means by which they both sought to transcend their creaturely limits and ascend into the heights where they could enjoy godlike attributes, including the right to make the rules defining "good and evil." It is abundantly clear that women have no corner on an inordinate lust for godlike powers and uninhibited, self-willed autonomy.

In his analysis of the origin of sin, Paul breaks with traditional rabbinic exposition of the Fall and holds Adam, rather than Eve, responsible: "Therefore, just as sin came into the world through one man, and death came through sin, and so death spread to all because all have sinned" (Rom. 5:12; see 1 Cor. 15:21ff.). Paul never mentions Eve as having anything to do with the Fall. While Eve may have been deceived, Adam was not. His sin was greater because it was a knowing and deliberate action of the will.

THE CURSE

For those seeking to justify gender hierarchy, invariably they cite God's curse upon the woman: "To the woman he said, 'I will greatly increase your pangs in childbearing; in pain you shall bring forth children, yet your desire shall be for your husband, **and he shall rule over you'**" (Gen. 3:16, emphasis added).

What is of vital importance to note, however, is that **man's domination over woman is part of the curse of sin after the Fall** and does not represent God's original intention for male-female relationships! It is a prediction of the consequences of the Fall, rather than a prescription of God's ideal order. Also, the statement describes man's aggressive action as one who will overpower and dominate the woman. The woman's submission is not voluntary but forced. If the curse is taken as representing a new and permanent divine decree as to how men and women are to relate to each other, then we would be duty-bound to treat all parts of the curse in the same manner: that is, women are forbidden to use anesthetic or modern gynecological techniques to decrease their pain in childbirth. Likewise, men are prohibited from devising any sort of technology to ease their toil in wresting a living from the soil. To do so would be to violate a divine mandate to "toil" and "sweat" (Gen. 3:17, 19).

Since no interpreter insists that all parts of the curse are binding in perpetuity, it is purely arbitrary to focus upon one part of the curse and universalize it as an eternally established decree governing male-female relationships in perpetuity. A consistent dimension of God's revelation of himself, throughout the Scriptures, is that neither judgment nor curse will have the last word. What began in grace (creation) will end in grace (redemption). We see this wonderfully demonstrated in the promise included in the curse directed to the serpent: "I will put enmity between you and the woman, and between your offspring and hers; **he will strike your head,** and you will strike his heel" (Gen. 3:15, emphasis added).

The good news of the protevangelium—the prophecy of salvation—is that from woman will come a Savior who will smash the serpent and liberate humankind from the bondage of sin. Through one woman's deception sin made its entrance into the world: by another woman's obedience the Savior was born into the world. Through one woman the shadow of the curse fell upon all: through another woman the shadow of the curse is lifted for all (Gal. 3:10-13). Yet it was through the "seed" of the woman under the curse that the messianic line was preserved until the coming of Jesus Christ. As Aida Spencer notes, "The very seed which bruises the serpent becomes the seed which saves Eve."[14]

As a final touch of grace, we note that "the Lord God made garments of skin for Adam and his wife, and clothed them" (Gen. 3:21, NASB). God himself offered up the life of an animal in order that the man and the woman He had made might be clothed with the "garments of righteousness" and that they might once again stand before Him, without shame, in a relationship of intimate union and holy communion. Even as both were one in creation and one in responsibility for the Fall, so now both are one in redemption. We have here a clear prefigurement of the exalted vision of the apostle Paul when he describes believers, "male and female," as "all . . . one in Christ Jesus" (Gal. 3:28).

THE BITTER CONSEQUENCES OF THE CURSE

Unfortunately, humankind chose not to live in the light of God's grace but in disobedience and thus under the shadow of the curse. Consequently, the man who was created to rule and have dominion over the earth became enslaved to the earth. And the woman who was formed to be a ruling helper "corresponding to the man" found herself under the domination of man. The intimacy and fellowship of mutuality gave way to the distance and tension inherent in all hierarchies. From this point onward, history played out this distortion of relationships in a rigid patriarchy of male supremacy that, in the main, debased women and dehumanized men. No matter what may be said in support of patriarchy, it institutionalizes discrimination against women. This sad consequence of the Fall is not glossed over in the Scriptures but is reported in starkly brutal detail. We can only cite a few examples.

Women's identity would always be dependent upon and defined by men: their fathers, husbands, and sons. Genealogies followed the male line. All social institutions were ruled by men. Only men could inherit property and carry on the family's name: hence, the urgency for every man to have a son (see the Levirate law of marriage, Deut. 25:5-10). If sons survived the father, neither the widow nor their daughters had any share in the inheritance.

Only males were regarded as true Israelites, and only males bore the mark of their religious identity in circumcision. Women were purchased and owned as a possession of their husbands. Their justification for viewing women as "possessions" was based upon the 10th commandment: "You shall not covet your neighbor's house; you shall not covet your neighbor's wife, or male or female slave, or ox, or donkey, or anything that belongs to your neighbor" (Exod. 20:17). House, slave, ox, donkey, and wife were all regarded as property of the husband.

Only the woman was required to be chaste until marriage and submit proof of her virginity on her wedding night. If she could not, the Law required her to be stoned to death. If a husband suspected his wife of unfaithfulness and a "spirit of jealousy" overcame him, the wife could be forced to undergo an "adultery test." She was brought to the priest who would write, on a scroll, a list of curses that would fall upon her if proven guilty. Then he would mix dirt from the tabernacle floor with water, dip the scroll in it, and make her drink it. If her abdomen swelled and her thigh wasted away, she was obviously guilty. If not, then she was absolved of guilt and would be able to bear children (Num. 5:11-31). There was no such adultery test, however, for husbands.

The social institution that not only permitted such dehumanizing treatment of women but gave to it the official sanction of legal and religious orthodoxy was patriarchalism. Webster defines it as the "social organization marked by the supremacy of the father in the clan or family, the legal dependence of wives and children, and the reckoning of descent and inheritance in the male line." Because the oneness between male and female was no longer affirmed or exhibited but was replaced by a gender-driven hierarchy, we can see how patriarchy not only debased women but demeaned the men who ruled over them.

For instance, to save his own skin when he journeyed to Egypt, Abraham lied to Pharaoh about Sarah, his wife, fully understanding that in doing so he would compromise her morally (Gen. 12:10-20). He repeated this shabby deception later with Abimelech (20:1-18), and his son Isaac followed suit (26:1-11). Neither Abraham nor Isaac demonstrated sacrificial love for their wives. To the contrary, God had to intervene to save both Sarah and Rebekah. Abraham used Hagar, Sarah's handmaiden, solely as a means of getting an heir—a "birth machine." Surrogate motherhood has a long history. When tension arose between Isaac and Ishmael, and consequently between their mothers, Abraham forced Hagar and her son from the security of his family and sent her into a barren wilderness with only a loaf of bread and a skin of water for sustenance. She and her son would have perished if an angel had not come to their rescue (21:8-21). Is there any wonder that the descendants of Ishmael, the Arabic peoples, and the descendants of Isaac, the Jews, have been intractable enemies ever since?

Even though Jacob was deceived into marrying Leah, and cared nothing for her, he continued to have relations with her because she was successful in bearing him many sons (Gen. 29:31ff.). Two wives were not enough for him; he also had children by Rachel's and Leah's maidservants. In a patriarchal society, women were valued primarily for purposes of procreation.

Nowhere is the low estimate of women more tragically demonstrated than in the sordid saga centering upon Lot, Abraham's nephew. When depraved men of Sodom demanded that he deliver over the two male guests in his home so that they might violate them homosexually, Lot offered up his two virgin daughters to be raped instead. Since he treated his daughters as sex objects, they returned the favor following the destruction of Sodom and Gomorrah, by having intercourse with him while he was drunk. Both bore him sons through this incestuous relationship. One became the progenitor of the Moabites and the other of the Ammonites, both bitter enemies who harassed the Israelites for centuries thereafter.

A similar incident occurred during the period of the judges when a Levite offered his concubine to the wicked men of Gibeah. They raped her so brutally that she died.

This in turn precipitated a civil war in which the tribe of Benjamin was almost exterminated (Judges 19—21).

Samson's womanizing led him to marry a Philistine woman whom he abruptly abandoned on their wedding night. When her father subsequently gave her to Samson's friend as a wife, he became so enraged that he went on a rampage destroying Philistine property. They in turn retaliated by burning Samson's former wife and her father to death. Samson was undone by another Philistine woman, Delilah, who was manipulated by the men in her life for their own nefarious purposes. It is clear that on both sides, women were treated as pawns to be used and abused at the whim of men.

There is so much that is praiseworthy about King David, but his relations with women are not. Though married to Saul's daughter, Michal, he took unto himself both Ahinoam and Abigail during his wilderness wanderings, then later added four more wives. We discover that these women were primarily important for their childbearing abilities when we note that their identity is secondary to that of their sons (2 Sam. 3:2-5). When David came to power as king, he demanded that Michal, his former wife, be brought to him, despite the fact that she was, by this time, married to Paltiel, who was an unusual husband in that he followed her weeping all the way to David's palace (vv. 12-16). And what of Michal? Not only was she taken unwillingly from a caring husband, but she sank into oblivion as just another member of David's growing harem (5:13-16). No wonder she despised David when she saw him dancing naked in the streets. For this lack of respect, David punished her by depriving her of the ancient world's most important female status symbol: "And Michal the daughter of Saul had no child to the day of her death" (6:23; cf. vv. 16-23).

Not content with his many wives and concubines, David's eyes lit up with lust when he spied Bathsheba. In the historic manner of men who have no regard for the rights or feelings of women, he forcibly seized her, got her pregnant, and then deliberately arranged for the murder of her husband. It is interesting to note that God disciplined David and not Bathsheba. He was not allowed to justify rape by blaming the woman for being attractive, as is too sadly the case in our judicial system today.

Absalom's actions were indicative of the way women were viewed in ancient Israel. When he seized the throne from David, he showed his disdain for his father by having intercourse with his father's concubines on the palace roof in full view of the people, with no regard whatsoever for the hapless women (2 Sam. 16:20-22). Another of David's sons, Amnon, raped his half-sister, Tamar, and David showed no emotion—no outrage at the violation done her. However, when he learned that his rebellious son, Absalom, had been killed in battle, he wept loudly with bitter tears (18:33). Furthermore, when David returned to the palace after Absalom's rebellion had been put down, "the king took the ten women, the concubines whom he had left to keep the house, and placed them under guard and provided them with sustenance, but did not go in to them. So they were shut up until the day of their death, living as widows" (20:3, NASB)—as if it was their fault they had been raped and shamed by Absalom! Blaming the victim was not invented in the 20th century. This kind of despicable treatment of women, even one's own wives and daughters, was not regarded as reprehensible in a patriarchal society where women existed solely for the pleasure and purposes of men.

It is not surprising, then, that David's son Solomon followed in his father's footsteps. He took unto himself 700 wives and 300 concubines. In his day these served as status symbols of both his wealth and his sexual prowess. As absolute monarch he had the power to collect as many women as he wanted, and the women involved were powerless to deny him. Once the principle of patriarchy was given religious sanction and social approval, there remained few external controls to prevent demeaning, debasing, and abusive treatment of women. As we see so clearly in Solomon's case, in the process of using and thus degrading women with impunity, he in turn was corrupted by them: "As Solomon grew old, his wives turned his heart after other gods" (1 Kings 11:4, NIV).

It may seem that these examples are isolated and atypical. Yet we are hard-pressed to find even one husband-wife relationship in the Old Testament that approximates the lofty ideal voiced by Paul when he wrote, "Husbands, love your wives, just as Christ loved the church and gave himself up for her" (Eph. 5:25). There is, however, one marvelous example of genuine love and deep friendship in the Old Testament between two people. A long chapter is devoted to chronicling it in all of its lofty sentiment and tender emotion. The sad fact, however, is that it does not occur between a husband and a wife but between a man and another man: David and Jonathan (1 Samuel 20). Patriarchalism made it virtually impossible for a man to enjoy true fellowship with his wife because of the inferior and subordinate position in which it placed her.

Patriarchalism deprived both the male and the female of the wonderful human gift of friendship they were created by God to bestow on each other, because instead of a horizontal relationship of equality and mutuality, it forced them into a vertical relationship of master and slave. Gretchen Gaebelein Hull rightly observes that in patriarchalism "women cease to be partners in a 'one flesh' union and become possessions, treated as objects to be picked up or discarded at the will of the men who control their destinies. Perpetuating the family or the clan or even the institution of patriarchy itself becomes the overriding consideration, not justice—and certainly not the human rights of women."[15]

GREAT WOMEN OF THE BIBLE

In spite of the nearly universal subjugation of women to men in ancient Israel, faithfully documented in the Old Testament, the Hebrew Scriptures also celebrate a large number of women who transcended their lowly status and were recognized for great faith and exploits in their own right.[16] The roll call begins with Sarah who is mentioned 35 times in the Book of Genesis alone. The heir through whom "all the families of the earth shall be blessed" (12:3) comes equally through Abraham and Sarah. To Abraham the promise of a son is given, but to Sarah the "miracle child" is born. Both male and female are necessary for the realization of God's covenantal blessing to all generations. Both Abraham and Sarah are eulogized by Paul and the author of Hebrews as models of faith (Romans 4; Hebrews 11).

A great deal of attention is devoted to securing just the right wife for Isaac, the "son of promise." Neither Isaac's wife, Rebekah, nor his son Jacob's wife, Rachel, were passive personalities but actively involved in carrying out the purposes of God through His people. Both are honored in the New Testament. Miriam, Moses' and Aaron's older sister, played a key role in the dramatic events associated with the Exodus. Miriam may have saved Moses' life when she stepped out of the shadows after Pharaoh's daughter discovered him hidden along the bank of the Nile and offered to find a nurse for the baby. By securing his own mother, Jochebed, for this task, she guaranteed that Moses would not only enjoy all of the privileges of being raised in Pharaoh's court but also come to know and value his racial origins and religious heritage. This prepared him for the epic role he was to play in leading the children of Israel out of Egyptian bondage and establishing them as a "holy nation" to the Lord their God. Miriam is the first prophetess and poet mentioned in Scripture. She was also an accomplished musician who led Israel in a great post-Exodus celebration. Though she became involved in petty jealousy and criticism of her brother's leadership, she repented, was forgiven, and was restored to honor. Tradition indicates that Israel mourned her passing for 30 days.

Rahab, an Amorite harlot, exhibited great faith in Israel's God when she sheltered the two spies sent by Joshua into Canaan. She and her family were spared the destruction of Jericho. She became the wife of Salmon, one of the two spies. To her was born Boaz who married Ruth. Their son, Obed, became the father of Jesse, the father of David. Not only did God choose a woman to become a link in the royal line through whom Jesus would be born, but a most unlikely one: a Gentile harlot. In such a rigidly patriarchal culture, it is worth noting that four women are included in the lineage of Jesus: two were non-Israelites, Rahab and Ruth, and the other two were involved in moral irregularity, Tamar and Bathsheba (Matt. 1:1-11).

Deborah, a prophetess and a poet, became the first female ruler in Israel's history—and one of the first in antiquity. When Barak's heart failed him for fear, it was Deborah who led the Israelites into battle against Sisera's hordes. She judged Israel so well for 40 years that she was honored with the title "a mother in Israel." Jael, the Jewish maiden who drove a tent spike through Sisera's head, may well be described as the first to strike a mighty blow for women's liberation.

Huldah, a later prophetess, was consulted when the lost book of the Law of God was found in the Temple. She was the one whom Josiah sought out, rather than any male priest or prophet, to validate the authenticity of the scroll.

Her prophetic message, followed by the public reading of the Law, precipitated the first great spiritual revival and social reform in Israel's history. Arlene Swidler observes:

> This marks the first time any of the Hebrew scriptures were officially recognized as authentic. Josiah's acknowledgement of the Book of the Law, then, represents the first beginnings of our biblical canon. And the authority to pass judgment on this initial entry into the canon was given to a woman. At the beginning of the Bible we find Huldah; in her we discover the first scriptural authority, the founder of biblical studies. . . . The early church recognized her greatness. The prayer for the ordination of a deaconess in the *Apostolic Constitutions* (4th century A.D.) begins: "Oh eternal God, the Father of our Lord Jesus Christ, the Creator of man and of woman, who didst replenish with the Spirit Miriam and Deborah, and Anna, and Huldah."[17]

Many other women played key roles in Israel's salvation history, such as Hannah, Samuel's mother, and Esther, whose devotion to her people and personal heroism averted the total destruction of her people. It is ironic, and marvelous, that out of a patriarchal culture, so heavily weighted on the side of men, two books praising the faith and exploits of women not only were canonized as sacred Scripture but carry the women's names as well: Ruth and Esther.

We can summarize our overview of women in the Hebrew Scriptures as follows: first, women are coequal with men in all respects by way of God's creative intention. Second, disequilibrium entered the world through sin for which both the man and the woman are held equally responsible. Third, patriarchy, with its dominance-subordination hierarchy, entered the world as a consequence of sin and in no way represents either God's original or final intentions as to how men and women are to relate to each other. Further, patriarchy inevitably led to the devaluation and dehumanization of women, which in turn deprived men of the full measure of fellowship and companionship that they were created to enjoy. Finally, the Scriptures faithfully record the story of many women who rose above the narrow confines of culturally imposed subjugation and became heroes in their exploits for God and their people.

· 4

Jesus and Women

*I*t is surely a fact of inexhaustible significance that "when the fullness of time had come, God sent his Son, born of a woman" (Gal. 4:4), entirely without the participation of a man—that is, if we take the doctrine of the Virgin Birth seriously.[1] God created the first Adam out of the dust of the earth but brought forth the Second Adam out of the living flesh of the woman (Rom. 5:12-21). The curse upon Eve and her daughters was lifted through the obedience of Mary and her Son. The seed of the woman, Eve, had come to smash the head of the serpent and deliver all humankind from the tyranny of the law of sin and death. No race or class of human beings have ever been more enslaved by the Law than women.

Luke celebrates the birth of Christ as a cosmic event of epic importance, a divine act of historic magnitude. The angel Gabriel revealed himself to a humble Jewish peasant maiden with this salutation, "Greetings, favored one! The Lord is with you. . . . for you have found favor with God" (Luke 1:28, 30). Her cousin Elizabeth echoed the angel's word when she greeted Mary, "Blessed are you among women, and blessed is the fruit of your womb" (v. 42). Mary anticipated the new status that this gracious intervention of God bestowed upon her as a woman, and by extension upon all women, by exclaiming in the Magnificat:

"My soul magnifies the Lord, and my spirit rejoices in God my Savior, for he has looked with favor on the lowliness of his servant. Surely, from now on **all generations will call me blessed**" (vv. 46-48, emphasis added).

If all women are bound under Eve's curse, why then are not all released under Mary's blessing? How could we ever imagine that God would trust to a woman the birth, care, and nurture of His only begotten Son and yet deny her full freedom to proclaim the gospel of that very same Son?

In His first sermon delivered in the synagogue of His hometown, Nazareth, Jesus was handed a scroll. It was the Book of Isaiah. He turned until He found exactly the right passage for His keynote address. It was to become His "Emancipation Proclamation," which would unleash the greatest spiritual and social revolution in the history of humankind. The freedom it announced and envisioned for all peoples had dawned with His coming but is yet to be realized in all of its fullness. Nevertheless, its impact is just now being felt in full measure, particularly in reference to the release of women from bondage to inferiority and servility. Jesus took the scroll and read: "The Spirit of the Lord is upon me, because he has anointed me to bring good news to the poor. He has sent me to proclaim release to the captives and recovery of sight to the blind, to let the oppressed go free, to proclaim the year of the Lord's favor" (Luke 4:18-19).

Luke records that "the eyes of all in the synagogue were fixed on him" (4:20). No wonder! Clearly, something new was at hand that would be dangerous to the old. On the one hand, there was promise in the gospel of liberation that would set all captives free. At last all of God's children would stand on level ground before Him and in relation to one another.

On the other hand, there was also a threat inherent in such a revolutionary program: namely, all hierarchies depend, in some measure, upon having someone to rule or to dominate. If the poor suddenly realize they, too, are fellow heirs of all the privileges and benefits of the kingdom of God, and begin to claim their rightful share in it now, what alarming social upheaval might occur? If the ignorant masses, accustomed to unquestioning passivity before the "authorities," suddenly experience a recovery of spiritual sight and intellectual independence, how long could existing repressive political and religious structures survive? If all captives are suddenly set free, what would it mean to the economic interests of those who depend upon an enslaved peoples for their sustenance? If the sleeping giant of oppressed peoples were to awaken and stir to life, would tyrants and despots be able to maintain their lock upon power and privilege? And if women, so long bound by chains of subordination and servitude, should suddenly claim equal rights with men granted to them by God in creation, what would become of man's control over marriage, the home, the family, the workplace, and the nation? What dislocation and disruption might occur if this "theology of liberation" were to be taken seriously?

The male listeners in that Nazareth synagogue found their initial enthusiasm for Jesus' sermon blunted considerably when He eulogized—horror of horrors!—a woman (Luke 4:25-26). Furthermore, the woman at Zarephath was a widow: a woman without a husband, a virtual nonperson, someone not worth mentioning in public, much less in a sermon. And if that wasn't scandal enough, the particular woman Jesus chose to use, as an illustration of the magnanimity of God's grace, was a non-Israelite, a pagan Sidonian! To top it off, Jesus suggested that God's love and tender healing mercies extend not only to Jews but also to Gentiles, even Naaman the leper (v. 27), whose repulsive disease was itself regarded as a curse from God. That was the last straw! The righteous citizens of Jesus' hometown seized Him and dragged Him to the brow of the hill on which Nazareth was built. And they would have thrown Him off the cliff to His death if He had not somehow "passed through their midst" (v. 30, NASB).

We are not surprised to learn that very early in His ministry "the Pharisees went out and immediately began taking counsel with the Herodians against Him, as to how they might destroy Him" (Mark 3:6, NASB). They perceived, correctly, that Jesus of Nazareth—this untutored and unordained, self-proclaimed prophet—represented a threat of grave magnitude to the status quo. He cut across the grain—and dangerously so. If this new wine of liberation and equality got out of hand, it might destroy the old wineskins of established social structures and cherished religious traditions.

Their fears were well-founded. Nowhere do we see this more clearly than in how Jesus challenged, in precept and by example, institutions that devalued and oppressed women. We do not find in Him any expression whatsoever of the demeaning and shabby way in which Jewish males treated women in His day. To the contrary, He always treated them with utmost dignity and respect. He neither ignored nor patronized them. He did not deal with them as females but as human beings. Unlike the "bleeding Pharisees," so named because they closed their eyes at the approach of a woman and thus kept bumping into things, Jesus conversed and socialized as naturally with women as with men. He taught that they were choice and chosen daughters of the most high God. Women were locked out of the synagogue, but they were welcome wherever Jesus was and whenever He taught. He was as sensitive to the needs of an abhorrent, hemorrhaging woman who touched the hem of His garment as to those of a prestigious synagogue ruler whose daughter was sick unto death. Women were among His closest friends and most devoted followers. He and the disciples depended upon them largely for their support. Women were the last at the Cross and the first to the Tomb. That a rabbi, a teacher, would welcome women disciples and followers was unheard of in His day.

According to both Mark and Luke's chronology of Jesus' ministry, His second sermon, preached at Capernaum, was interrupted by a man with a demon who cried out, "Ha! What do we have to do with You, Jesus of Nazareth? Have you come to destroy us?" (Luke 4:34, NASB). As the miracle story unfolds, the answer is an unequivocal "Yes!" Jesus came to break the chains of demonic oppression and set the captives free (see vv. 31-36 and Mark 1:21-28). This is immediately followed by Jesus doing something unprecedented in proper Jewish society. He, a Jewish male, went into the inner chamber of a house where a woman, Peter's mother-in-law, lay sick with a fever. He rebuked the fever: "And she immediately arose and waited on them" (Luke 4:39, NASB). The Greek word for "wait" is *diakonia*, a verb form of the noun *diakonos*, "servant."

In an astonishing reversal of all accepted social norms, Jesus rejected all titles that in any way suggested rule, dominance, or authority and deliberately chose, instead, *diakonos*, "servant" (Mark 10:42-45; cf. Phil. 2:5-9). In so doing He elevated "servant," minister, as the loftiest and most exalted title that any of His followers could ever claim. And so in these two opening miracles in the ministry of Jesus, we see something deeper is going on. By violating social convention, Jesus demonstrates that He intends to challenge and break the chains that bind people to demonic spirits and oppressive social structures. A woman, even as a man, can be "raised up" by Jesus and set free to become a *diakonos*, a "servant," a "minister" unto Him and for Him.

According to John's chronology, Jesus' ministry begins in Cana of Galilee at a wedding feast where Jesus turns water into wine (2:1-11). Little did those celebrants realize what kind of new wine Jesus would pour into marriage and family life, destroying the old hierarchy of dominion and subordination and introducing a whole new estimate of relationships built upon mutual submission and self-giving love. Jesus would begin the process in many ways, including His penetrating critique of divorce laws, which were especially unjust and damaging in their disposal of wives. Paul would finish it in his revolutionary exposition of Kingdom relationships and how they are to work within the marriage union (Eph. 5:18-33). John notes: "This beginning of His signs Jesus did in Cana of Galilee, and manifested His glory, and His disciples believed in Him" (2:11, NASB). It is hard to imagine how the disciples could have seen much "glory" under the old system of domination and subservience in marriage. The disciples must have seen something new in the way Jesus approached marriage that day, which excited their imaginations and won their hearts.

Jesus not only violated rabbinic tradition but offended Martha's sense of propriety when He permitted Mary to hear the Word. When Martha complained that Mary was not fulfilling her proper domestic role in the kitchen, He defended her: "Mary has chosen the good part, which shall not be taken away from her" (Luke 10:42, NASB). In so doing, **Jesus affirmed the right of women to hear God's Word!** In His gentle rebuke, Jesus was stating a new principle that would break the autocracy of women's culturally and socially imposed role: namely, **it is more important for women to attend to the Word of God than it is to fulfill household duties.** A woman is greater than what she does. She has worth and dignity apart from childbearing. Her status is not dependent on her relationship to a man but is dependent on her relationship to God. She is *adam, anthropos,* a human being in her own right, worthy of the Master's full and undivided attention.

Jesus scandalized His own disciples by spending a lunch hour talking to a woman, a despised Samaritan woman, and a morally disreputable woman at that! No self-respecting rabbi would stoop to speak with any woman in public, much less talk theology! Yet it was to this most unlikely of all women that Jesus first disclosed himself as the Messiah of God. He spoke of truth vast and profound, such as woman's ears never before heard from the lips of a man. He taught her that God is a Spirit and that He is no respecter of persons or national boundaries. It is ironic—and wonderful—that **it was not a Jew, not even a man, but a Gentile woman who became the first preacher of the gospel.** Through this woman's witness, Samaria was opened up to the ministry of Jesus, which, in turn, prepared the way for a great revival under the post-Pentecost preaching of Philip, Peter, and John (Acts 8:12-17).

Jesus enjoyed a special friendship with Mary and Martha and their brother, Lazarus. It was to Martha, a disciple and special friend, that Jesus disclosed himself as "the resurrection and the life. Those who believe in me, even though they die, will live" (John 11:25). John's Gospel does not record Peter's confession of faith but rather Martha's: "Yes, Lord, I believe that you are the Messiah, the Son of God" (v. 27).

Jesus accommodated His teaching to women by referring to objects and situations with which they were most familiar, such as wedding feasts, lost coins, grinding corn, putting yeast in bread, bearing children. By taking children into His arms and blessing them, He was assuming more of a maternal than a paternal role as it was practiced in that day.

Jesus broke protocol by freely conversing with women. His healing touch brought release to a woman crippled for 18 years. In a religious culture where Jewish males were regularly identified as "sons of Abraham," Jesus calls her a "daughter of Abraham," much to the indignation of the synagogue official (Luke 13:10-17). Jesus did not recoil in horror when a ceremonially unclean woman touched the hem of His garment. On another occasion He shocked His host, a Pharisee, and the other male guests by allowing a woman of disrepute to anoint His feet with perfume and wipe them with her hair. Rather than rebuke her, Jesus turned the occasion into an opportunity to teach a wonderful lesson about the grace of God. The miracle-story concludes with Jesus saying to this woman what He also said to the woman who touched the hem of His garment, "Your faith has saved you; go in peace" (7:50; see vv. 36-50). Women, even the immoral and ritually unclean, are capable of exercising saving faith and receiving the unconditional forgiveness of Christ. In so doing, He broke the chains of social isolation that had cut them off from respectable society, and He gave back to them dignity and respect as "children of God," a right that was theirs by election, creation, and redemption.

Nowhere is Jesus' concern for women more powerfully portrayed than in His strong and uncompromising teaching on divorce. In the Sermon on the Mount Jesus states: "But I say to you that anyone who divorces his wife, except on the ground of unchastity, causes her to commit adultery" (Matt. 5:32). How is it that a man, by divorcing his wife, forces her into a life of immorality? The answer lies in reminding ourselves of the handicaps a woman faced in that culture. What was a woman to do to support herself when turned out of house and home, especially considering she was illiterate and untrained for anything except domestic duties? To keep body and soul together and support her daughters who were often expelled with her, there were only two options open to her: one was to sell her body as a prostitute and the other was to bind herself into someone else's household as a bondslave, which amounted to the same thing since masters had absolute rights over the bodies of their female servants.

So when Jesus warned that "whoever divorces his wife and marries another commits adultery against her" (Mark 10:11), He was striking a mighty blow on behalf of women's rights. No longer would two sets of standards apply. If the husband forced his wife into immorality, he was likewise guilty of an immoral act for which he would be held accountable. Women were not to be used, abused, and cast aside. Women were not to be treated as objects!

Likewise, Jesus confronts the devaluation and depersonalization of women head-on when He says, "You have heard that it was said, 'You shall not commit adultery.' But I say to you that everyone who looks at a woman with lust has already committed adultery with her in his heart" (Matt. 5:27-28). The "lustful look" is synonymous with "coveting," which is forbidden in the 10th commandment (Exod. 20:17), because it dehumanizes a woman and turns her into an object to be toyed with and possessed for men's selfish gratification. How should men treat women? The answer is found in the 5th commandment, "Honor your father and your mother" (v. 12). Even as a man holds his mother in the highest esteem and regards her with the utmost respect, so should all women be treated (see Mark 7:10; 10:19). Women are no longer to be used, abused, and discarded but must be accorded all of the dignity and honor that befits daughters of the most high God.

In the case of the woman taken in adultery (John 8:1-11), Jesus set himself against not only the male chauvinists of His day but the law of Moses itself. The law to which the Pharisees referred called for stoning both the man and the woman caught in an adulterous act (Lev. 20:10; Deut. 22:22-27). That only the woman was brought to Him reveals the double standard operative in Jesus' day: namely, men were exempted but women were expendable. By saving this woman's life, Jesus laid down the radically new principle that **women are more important than the Mosaic law!** When Jesus said to her, "Neither do I condemn you" (John 8:11), He set her free from the double curse of being born a daughter of Eve and the guilt of being drawn into immoral behavior. Furthermore, when He said, "Go, and sin no more" (v. 11, KJV), He thereby declared that she had the potential of living a holy life and of fully reflecting the beautiful face of God in whose image she was created. "She whom the Son sets free shall be free indeed" (John 8:32, paraphrased).

While one disciple betrayed Him, another denied Him, and the rest fled into the darkness leaving Jesus to walk the last mile of His earthly journey alone, women followed Him to the Cross and beyond. They were not ashamed to identify themselves with one who was condemned as a religious heretic and crucified as a political subversive. They did not shrink from putting themselves in harm's way by staying at the Cross until the bitter end. They loved Him with a devotion that knew no bounds.

Luke, who is the only Gentile to author biblical books, must have been especially impressed by Jesus' extraordinary attitude toward, and treatment of, women. As he writes his Gospel, he demonstrates the impartiality by which Jesus dealt with both men and women by consistently linking stories about men with stories about women. Such pairings can be found in almost every chapter of his Gospel and the Book of Acts. His Gospel opens with angelic announcements both to Zechariah and to Mary (1:5-38). He records both Mary's and Zechariah's songs of praise (vv. 46-79). Both Simeon and Anna bless the Christ child (2:25-

38). In His first sermon Jesus refers to two Gentiles: a Sidonian widow and Naaman the leper. Likewise, Jesus' first two miracles involve a man and a woman: the demoniac and Peter's mother-in-law (4:31-39). Luke names not only the male disciples but the female as well (6:12-19; 8:1-3).

Jesus' healing of the centurion's servant and raising up the widow's son are linked (7:1-17). Jesus pronounces the Word of forgiveness on behalf of both the paralytic and the prostitute (5:18-26; 7:36-50). After exorcising the Gerasene demoniac, Jesus heals the hemorrhaging woman and raises Jairus' daughter (8:26-56). The parable of the good Samaritan is followed by Jesus being entertained in the home of Mary and Martha (10:29-42). Jesus fields three questions about discipleship, including one from a woman (10:25—11:13). Those who will rise to accuse Israel include both the Ninevites and the queen of the south (11:29-36). Jesus straightens a bent-over woman and heals a man with dropsy (13:10-17; 14:1-6).

Luke relates two of Jesus' parables, one about a man who plants a mustard seed and another about a woman hiding leaven (13:18-21). He places two more of Jesus' parables side by side, one about a man searching for his lost sheep and another about a woman searching for her lost coin (15:1-10). Jesus talks about two men sleeping and two women grinding corn (17:32-35). He relates two examples of prayer: one involving a widow, and the other a Pharisee and a publican (18:1-14). After His warning against the hypocrisy of the scribes, Jesus draws attention to the widow who gave her all (20:45—21:4). On His way to the Cross, Jesus is assisted by Simon of Cyrene and lamented by women (23:26-31). Joseph of Arimathea begs for the body of Jesus, and the women from Galilee follow as it is laid in the tomb (vv. 50-56). Women are among those who stand at the foot of the Cross (v. 49). After His resurrection Jesus appears to women as well as to men (chap. 24).

Luke carries on that sensitivity to the role and importance of women in his account of the Early Church, where he often links women together with men. Women waited with the men in Jerusalem for the promised Holy Spirit (Acts 1:12-14). Peter proclaims that the promised Spirit will be poured out upon men and women and that both shall prophesy (2:17-18). The tragic story of Ananias's and Sapphira's deception is told, with the husband succumbing to the same judgment as his wife (5:1-11). Luke is careful to point out that great numbers of both men and women were being constantly added to the Church (v. 14).

Women must have been effective evangelists, for Luke records that Saul of Tarsus pursued and persecuted both "men and women" (Acts 8:3; 9:2). Philip baptized men and women believers in Samaria (8:12). Peter cured a lame man and then raised up a woman (9:32-43). When Paul preached at Antioch in Asia Minor, not only did leading men of the city rise up to throw him out, but devout Jewish women did as well (13:50). Paul began his ministry in Lystra by healing a lame man, and in Philippi by curing a demon-possessed girl (14:8-18; 16:16-34). Paul's first convert in Philippi was Lydia, who joined with the jailer in establishing the church there (vv. 14-15, 25-34). In Thessalonica, a great number of Greek men and leading women were persuaded to join Paul (17:1-4). Likewise, in Berea, both Greek men and women examined the Scriptures daily to see whether Paul's message was true, and they became believers (vv. 10-12). In Athens, Dionysius the Areopagite and a woman named Damaris were among the believers (v. 34). Aquila, and his wife, Priscilla, became his hosts and coworkers at Corinth (18:1-4). Not only is Agabus the prophet mentioned, but also mentioned are Philip's four daughters who were prophetesses (21:9-10). Luke is careful to note that after his imprisonment, Paul makes his defense and shares his testimony with both Felix and Drusilla, and later with both Agrippa and Bernice (24:24; 25:13, 23; 26:30).

Luke makes it abundantly clear that, because of Christ, all walls separating race, social class, and gender are being torn down within the Body of Christ. Women, as well as men, are recipients of the grace of God and equally share in all aspects of life together in the church. So when Paul wrote that "there is no longer Jew or Greek, there is no longer slave or free, there is no longer male and female; for all of you are one in Christ Jesus" (Gal. 3:28), he was not envisioning an age yet to come but was describing what was already the case in the earliest Church as it lived out the teachings and example of Jesus.

Clearly, women have never had a greater champion, a mightier "liberationist," than Jesus of Nazareth. In word and deed, Jesus struck the chains that had for so long bound women in a demeaning state of depersonalized and dehumanized subordination and set them free to claim their inheritance as choice and chosen daughters of the most high God.

The release of the captives, promised by Jesus at the beginning of His ministry (Luke 4:18), is powerfully dramatized at the close of His ministry in the Temple-cleansing incident (Matt. 21:12-16). Herod's Great Temple was built theologically: that is, it was designed in such a way that the unclean would not desecrate the holy of holies, wherein dwelt the living presence of God. To prevent this from happening, a series of four courts were built around it to protect it. The outer court was called the Court of the Gentiles, where sacrificial animals were sold and money was changed. Then came the Court of the Women, beyond which women could not go. Only Jewish males, in good health and having no deformities, could proceed to the Court of the Israelites to present sacrifices to the priests, who alone were allowed in the holy place. No one, however, was permitted behind the veil except the high priest on the Day of Atonement, and only after going through elaborate rituals of purification.

In the most dramatic move of His ministry, Jesus invaded the Temple, cast out those who were conducting business, and in the process tore down those walls that had for so long locked people out of experiencing the immediate presence of God. First, He invited Gentiles into the innermost courts of the Temple, citing Isa. 56:7, "My house shall be called a house of prayer **for all nations**" (NIV, emphasis added). Then He welcomed "the blind and the lame" (Matt. 21:14) into the Temple, those unfortunates who had been barred from any part of the Temple precincts because of the curse of their affliction (Lev. 21:17-23), and He healed them. Then He threw open the gates to children who began to sing, "Hosanna to the Son of David." Where there are children there are bound to be mothers close by. From this we are justified in assuming that Jesus opened the gates to the innermost courts of the Temple to women.

On the Cross, Jesus attacked the final barrier separating a holy God from His people, the great curtain protecting the holy of holies, which was approximately 60 feet long and 30 feet high, weighing as much as a ton. For when Jesus died, "the veil of the temple was torn in two from top to bottom" (Matt. 27:51, NASB). The author of Hebrews exults, "Since, then, we have a great high priest who has passed through the heavens, Jesus, the Son of God, . . . Let us therefore approach the throne of grace with boldness, so that we may receive mercy and find grace to help in time of need" (Heb. 4:14, 16). Everyone now has immediate access to God through Christ: Jew and Gentile, bond and free, male and female. Human hierarchies evaporate before His nondiscriminatory love and mercy. All are equally welcome. At last, all stand on level ground before Him.

Given the lowly status of women in Jesus' day, it is surely ironic that **the first Christian preachers of the Resurrection were not men, but women!** It was to the women who had come to the tomb early on that historic first day of the week that the angels first appeared. It was these women who first heard the good news, "Do not be afraid; I know that you are looking for Jesus who was crucified. He is not here; for he has been raised, as he said" (Matt. 28:5-6). It was to these same women that the first expression of the Great Commission was given: "Go quickly and tell His disciples that He has risen from the dead" (28:7, NASB). The disciples responded with disbelief at first and wrote the Resurrection Proclamation off as "an idle tale" (Luke 24:11). Not so the women: they not only believed without doubting but immediately began to broadcast the good news of Christ alive (Matt. 28:8). Three of the Gospels specifically mention that Jesus appeared, first of all, to women.

Since it would have been just as easy for the divine messengers to announce Christ's resurrection to the male disciples, huddled behind locked doors, we can only conclude that these post-Resurrection events, which focus so pointedly upon women, were by divine ordination. After centuries of being denied access to the Word of God, and being locked out of full access to the worship of God in Temple and synagogue, it is almost as if God were saying, "These are my beloved daughters, in whom I am well pleased. Listen to them!"

We conclude, therefore, that the time-worn practice of treating women as subhuman, relegating them to subservient roles, and denying them opportunity to preach, finds no support whatsoever in the example or teachings of Jesus. If we accept the Christological Principle of interpretation, the question of women's right to preach is settled right here in the affirmative.

One more objection to women preachers must be addressed: Why, then, did Jesus choose and send out on preaching missions only male apostles? The answer is apparent in what we now know about the limitations women faced in the first-century world. There was little chance that female apostles could have spearheaded the Great Commission, given the narrow social conventions of that day. For one thing, having been denied an education and access to the Hebrew Scriptures, it would have crippled their effort to prove that Jesus was the Messiah of God to unbelieving Jews. Furthermore, they would have been barred from preaching Christ in synagogues and would undoubtedly have been unable to gain a hearing in any public forum, especially from men. They would also have been unable to travel freely. Therefore, the predominance of male leaders in the disciple community had nothing to do with an eternally fixed divine decree but represented God's gracious accommodation of himself to the social structures and conventions of the world into which the gospel originally came.

Thanks to the seeds of liberation planted by Jesus and cultivated by Paul (as we shall see in the next chapter), women are increasingly enjoying the mature fruit of emancipation from gender discrimination and now enjoy an acceptance and freedom of movement never before known. Women today are as well educated as men. They have access to the best in biblical and theological training. They not only are accepted on an equal par with men in most public forums but are acknowledged leaders in all segments of the human enterprise as well. There is, therefore, no longer any justification for binding women under ancient cultural constraints that no longer apply. To do so is sheer prejudice and sexism.

In the same letter where Paul issued his revolutionary "emancipation proclamation" (Gal. 3:28), he also writes: "For freedom Christ has set us free. Stand firm, therefore, and do not submit again to a yoke of slavery" (5:1).

5·

Paul and Women

A cartoon appeared in a Christian magazine portraying Paul arriving by boat only to be met by a group of women carrying posters that read "Unfair to Women," "Paul Is a Male Chauvinist Pig." The caption underneath reports the sheepish apostle saying, "Heh, heh, I see you got my letter."[1]

When it comes to women's issues, the biblical storm inevitably centers upon Paul's letters. Maligned by feminists and lionized by traditionalists, Paul himself gets lost behind a barrage of claims and counterclaims. Unfortunately, most attention is focused upon those passages where he seems to severely restrict the role of women in church (1 Cor. 14:34-35; 1 Tim. 2:11-15), and where he appears to bind women under the traditional patriarchal domination of men (1 Cor. 11:2-9; Eph. 5:22; Col. 3:18). These "parts" are taken to be the "whole" of his teaching relative to women.

However, even a cursory glance at what he had to say about women and how he treated them leads us to the conclusion that, aside from Jesus, women have never had a more ardent advocate for full equality in home and church than he. Though raised and educated in a Jewish society that treated women as subhuman, he makes a radical departure from the narrow limits of his rabbinic training as "a Pharisee" (Phil. 3:5). In *The Apostle Paul and Women in the Church*,[2] Don Williams has engaged in a thorough study of every passage in Paul's letters where he speaks of women. It is astonishing to see how often Paul did refer to women and in what high esteem he held them. Such a study shatters stereotypes about Paul. Following Williams' lead, we will briefly survey some of what Paul has to say.

ROMANS

In his mighty letter to the Romans, his theological magnum opus, Paul sets forward his gospel of salvation by grace through faith: "The one who is righteous will live by faith" (1:17). While his main concern is to show that we are not justified by the works of the law but by faith in Jesus Christ, it is also his intention to show that the gospel of Jesus is universal in scope and transcends all racial, social, and gender barriers. It offers "salvation to everyone who believes, to the Jew first and also to the Greek" (v. 16, NASB). The gospel is the great leveler, particularly when it comes to artificial gender distinctions imposed by a patriarchal hierarchy, as we can see in the following examples.

In his analysis of man's descent into the abyss of sin, Paul speaks of both lesbians and homosexuals as equally under the wrath of God (1:26-27). This was a departure from rabbinical teaching, which placed greater weight upon the sin of the woman than upon the sin of the man.

Both Abraham and Sarah were equally impotent. Yet both equally believed the promise of God and equally shared in the subsequent joy over the birth of their son, Isaac (4:19-21). Along with the author of Hebrews, Paul celebrates Sarah as a model of great faith (Heb. 11:8-12).

When casting about for an appropriate way to illustrate freedom from the Law, Paul lifted up a wife—not a husband—as the paradigm of our new life in Christ and the freedom we are to enjoy in Him (7:1-3). If Paul had been true to his Pharisaic heritage, he would certainly have used a man, rather than a woman, as his model.

Paul deals with the complex issue of God's election of His people, Israel, in 9:1-26, and how the Church fits into this overall scheme. Not only did God choose a most unlikely people unto himself, but He chose most unlikely individuals within that people. More than that, Paul does something that was certain to scandalize the good Jewish males of his day: he draws attention to two women, Sarah and Rebekah, as special examples of the grace of God's surprising election. God was not at all averse to calling and utilizing women as vehicles for His revelation and as instruments in accomplishing His gracious purposes.

Most revealing is Paul's long list of greetings and commendations in the last chapter. First mentioned is not a man but a woman, Phoebe, to whom he entrusted the delivery of this letter to the Romans. In that most lists of names, then as now, began with those who were most prominent—such as "Peter, James, and John" heading the list of disciples, we can assume that Phoebe was held in the highest esteem both by Paul and by those to whom he wrote. He gives her an official recommendation as well as an endorsement of her ministry (cf. 2 Cor. 3:1-2), by addressing her as "our sister . . . a servant of the church which is at Cenchrea" (Rom. 16:1, NASB). Technically, "servant" is an accurate translation of the Greek word *diakonos*. Since Jesus deliberately rejected all leadership titles that implied positions of power and prestige and chose rather to define His role as *diakonos*, the apostles likewise always spoke of themselves, and of each other, as *diakonos*, "servants of the word" (Luke 1:2). Most English versions, however, translate *diakonos* as "minister" whenever it refers to apostles, pastors, and teachers—what we would call ordained clergy—in order to distinguish *diakonos* from its secular meaning, "to wait on tables" (Acts 6:2), and from "deacon," lay leaders in the church (1 Tim. 3:8-13).

When referring to Phoebe, however, most translators reveal their traditionalist bias by rendering *diakonos* as "servant" or "deaconess" because they cannot imagine a woman as a "minister." Such should not be the case. *Diakonos* appears in both masculine and feminine cases in the Greek, depending upon the gender of the one it modifies. In this instance, however, the rule is broken. *Diakonos* is masculine, even though it refers to a woman. It seems clear that Paul wants to communicate that Phoebe is more than someone who waits on tables. Neither is she a "deaconess," but just as much a full and respected minister of the Word as, for instance, Timothy or Titus, or even Paul himself.

Paul uses a second key word in describing Phoebe: "that you may welcome her in the Lord as is fitting for the saints, and help her in whatever she may require from you, for she has been a **benefactor** of many and of myself as well" (16:2, emphasis added). *Prostatis* can be translated as "helper" or "benefactor." While these words suggest an "assistant" in English, it is not the case in Greek. *Prostatis* literally means "one who stands in front or before." It is otherwise translated "to set over, to appoint with authority, to lead, protect, govern, preside, superintend, direct, rule, stand before others, set over others."[3] Phoebe was a benefactor because she was in a position of leadership where she could render an authoritative and effective ministry of the Word. In short, Paul commends Phoebe to the Romans because she was a minister—preacher, teacher, pastor—who was in charge (the pastor) "of the church which is at Cenchrea." The very fact that he encourages believers in Rome to "welcome her in the Lord as is fitting for the saints" indicates that there may have been some reluctance to submit to her ministry because she was a woman.

Paul greets "Prisca and Aquila, my fellow workers in Christ Jesus" (16:3, NASB). He does not greet Aquila as "my fellow worker," and his good wife, Prisca. Rather, he greets them as a husband-and-wife team. Word order is a significant factor in Greek grammar, with the emphasis falling on the words appearing first in a series or clause. Since, in this case, Paul mentions Prisca (Priscilla) first, this may indicate that she was the stronger leader of the two. Both equally shared in ministerial leadership of "the church that is in their house" (v. 5, NASB).

Paul greets "Mary, who has worked very hard among you" (16:6). The verb "work" or "labor," which he uses of Mary, is the same used elsewhere to speak of ministerial labor in the gospel. The prepositional phrase, "worked very hard for you," can also be rendered "worked hard over you" (see Gal. 4:11; 1 Thess. 5:12, NASB). Mary may well have had oversight of some important ministry in the church at Rome.

Paul greets "Andronicus and Junia [not "Junias," as the NASB and others render it], my relatives who were in prison with me; they are prominent among the apostles, and they were in Christ before I was" (16:7). In the earliest Greek manuscripts, Junia is rendered in the feminine case. Consequently, this may well have been another husband-and-wife team. What is of special interest is to note that both Andronicus and Junia were "in Christ" before Paul and "are prominent among the apostles." This is solid evidence that women were included in the wider apostolic circle by virtue of having seen the Lord, and Junia was prominent among them. There is support for this in the writings of the influential fourth-century Church father, Chrysostom, who commented on this verse by saying, "And indeed to be apostles at all is a great thing . . . Oh! how great is the devotion of this woman [Junia], that she should be even counted worthy of the appellation of apostle!"

"Greet Tryphaena and Tryphosa, workers in the Lord. Greet Persis the beloved, who has worked hard in the Lord" (16:12, NASB). As with Mary in verse 6, all three of these women were engaged in ministerial activity. Paul is not afraid to express deep-felt emotions of appreciation to women when he speaks of Persis as "beloved." The next verse also indicates his warm relations with women when he says, "Greet Rufus, a choice man in the Lord, also his mother and mine" (v. 13, NASB). Since Paul does not identify Rufus as his physical brother, he is probably indicating that Rufus' mother was like a mother to him. Paul greets two more women in verse 15, bringing the total to 9 women singled out for special mention in this list of 27 names. Historians know of no comparable list of greetings in antiquity that gives such a prominent place to women.

To summarize Paul's attitude toward women in Romans, we can draw these conclusions. First, men and women alike are under the sway of sin and the wrath of God, and both are equal recipients of the grace of salvation. Second, women as well as men have been chosen by God to play key roles in the unfolding of salvation history. Third, women shared equally, with men, in the work of Christian ministry. They exercised leadership roles in the earliest Church and may have even been numbered among the original apostolic circle. So there is, in his massive letter to the Romans, no suggestion whatsoever of women relegated to a secondary role of subordination or denied an active place of ministerial work and leadership in the church. In his view of women, Paul distanced himself radically from the traditional bias of his Jewish upbringing and rabbinical training.

1 CORINTHIANS

That the church at Corinth was a problem-plagued congregation should not blind us to the fact that it was also an innovative, dynamic, and exuberant community of new Christians. Never had the ancient world seen anything quite like it: a miscellaneous and unlikely collection of people bound together by a common confession of faith in Christ, and who were happily breaking cultural molds and shattering social strictures right and left. The walls that had separated Jew from Gentile for thousands of years were being torn down (1:22-25). The great social divide between rich and poor, mighty and humble, male and female was being bridged (vv. 26-29). Women, for so long locked out of participation in worship—except in the most extreme pagan cults—were welcomed alongside men and encouraged in the expression of their spiritual gifts (v. 7; 11:5; 12:4 ff.). No wonder that the apostle Paul, their spiritual father, greeted them with such warm affection and commendation (1:1-9) and took such pains to gently help them work through the issues that troubled them. A window is opened, in this detailed and multifaceted letter, for us to see how he applied his doctrine of full equality in Christ to women.

It is striking to note that a woman, rather than a man, was sent by the church at Corinth as the head of a delegation to inform Paul of what was going on: "For I have been informed concerning you, my brethren, by Chloe's people" (1:11, NASB). This is particularly noteworthy in that Paul also mentions that certain men had likewise come from Corinth, including Stephanas, Fortunatus, and Achaicus (16:17-18). This suggests that Chloe may have been held in higher esteem within the congregation than the men and was thereby entrusted with its deepest concerns.

In dealing with an infamous case of incest that involved a member of the Corinthian church (5:1-8), what is of interest is to note that Paul ignores the "father's wife" but comes down hard on the male offender. In so doing he was setting himself against rabbinical practice, which tended to absolve men while condemning women (cf. John 8:1-11). The redemptive purpose of church discipline is "that his spirit may be saved in the day of the Lord" (1 Cor. 5:5). That the offender repented is evident in that Paul later encourages the church to restore him to fellowship (2 Cor. 2:5-11).

In 6:15-16, Paul says that a believer who unites with a cult prostitute is "one body with her," thus denying Christ. This argument could be stated in the positive form as follows: the union of a man with his wife at once honors Christ and fulfills the purpose of human sexuality, which is the concrete physical expression of unity and equality between husband and wife.

In the middle of his letter, Paul writes one of the most astonishing tracts on marital relations to be found in antiquity (7:1-40). What is so revolutionary about it is that he treats husbands and wives as equals. This is evident in a symmetry of grammar and content that Paul consistently carries through in this chapter: "Let each man have his own wife, and let each woman have her own husband" (v. 2, NASB). This equality is evident in the next verses where he teaches that a wife has the same conjugal rights as her husband and that a man must not be insensitive to her needs—not even for such praiseworthy spiritual endeavors as prayer and fasting, unless she agrees, and then only for a short time (v. 5). His first word is directed to the man: "Let the husband fulfill his duty to his wife, and likewise also the wife to her husband. The wife does not have authority over her own body, but the husband does; and likewise also the husband does not have authority over his own body, but the wife does" (v. 4, NASB).

There is nothing remotely comparable to this in either the Old Testament or the voluminous tomes of rabbinic literature. In Jewish society a woman had no rights over her own body. She was entirely at the mercy of her husband's whims and desires, or lack thereof. Don Williams underscores the radicality of Paul's teaching and how it demolishes the very presupposition of male dominance and female subordination upon which the edifice of patriarchalism is built:

> This surprising expression of sexual equality and surrender again presupposes and defends the absolute equality of the sexes at their most intimate encounter. Each is to surrender his or her body to the other partner. Each is lord over the other's body. Paul presupposes that mutual love and self-giving will be expressed in our sexuality. No ego-trip, no will to power, no seduction or rape is tolerated. Here is mutual surrender. Here is the meeting of each other's sexual needs and desires. Here is tremendous freedom and joy in sexual union. Here is the physical expression of the one flesh (see 6:16). Here is the gospel in action—self-less love, giving to receive. The last thing in Paul's mind is male-dominance or egotism. . . . As Christ gave Himself for us, so we give ourselves for each other.[5]

Paul also affirms that a wife can be the spiritual leader of the home: "For the unbelieving husband is sanctified through his wife . . . for otherwise your children are unclean, but now they are holy" (7:14, NASB). Likewise, if a situation becomes intolerable, he gives permission for a wife to divorce her abusive, unbelieving husband without guilt, for "the sister is not under bondage in such cases" (v. 15, NASB). In both instances, Paul grants to the wife "equal rights," which she had previously been denied in both Jewish and Gentile society.

Paul reveals not only that the apostles were married but also that their spouses accompanied them on their missionary travels (9:3-5). Because it was uncommon for wives to travel with their husbands, Paul's reference here demonstrates the radical cultural shifts that were going on within the earliest Church and also underscores the value of companionship and mutual assistance afforded the apostles by their spouses.

When we come to chapter 11, we are faced with a problem. It appears that Paul reverses himself and reverts back to affirming a patriarchal hierarchy, a "chain of command," in which the woman is subordinate to the man. This passage is appealed to so frequently in submissionism literature that we need to get it before us.

> But I want you to understand that Christ is the head of every man, and the husband is the head of his wife, and God is the head of Christ. Any man who prays or prophesies with something on his head disgraces his head, but any woman who prays or prophesies with her head unveiled disgraces her head—it is one and the same thing as having her head shaved. For if a woman will not veil herself, then she should cut off her hair; but if it is disgraceful for a woman to have her hair cut off or to be shaved, she should wear a veil. For a man ought not to have his head veiled, since he is the image and reflection of God; but woman is the reflection of man. Indeed, man was not made from woman, but woman from man. Neither was man created for the sake of woman, but woman for the sake of man. For this reason a woman ought to have a symbol of authority on her head, because of the angels (11:3-10).

The problems to which Paul now addresses himself are those of proper decorum and conduct in public services. The break between chapters 10 and 11 should begin earlier where Paul lays down a basic principle that guides him now as he addresses himself to issues having to do with public worship (10:32—14:40). He begins the major section on worship by saying, "Give no offense either to Jews or to Greeks or to the church of God" (10:32, NASB). He concludes in the same manner: "But let all things be done properly and in an orderly manner" (14:40, NASB). The issue before him is not male-female relationships but appropriate behavior when they gather together as a body for worship.

Chapter 11 begins on a positive note: "Now I praise you because you . . . hold firmly to the traditions, just as I delivered them to you" (v. 2, NASB). What traditions? He mentions at least two in this letter: the first has to do with the proper celebration of the Lord's Supper (vv. 23-30), and the second deals with the central core of the gospel—Christ's death and resurrection—which he "delivered" to them (15:1-8). In other words, he has no problem with the *content* of their theology but only with the *form* of their worship. It is in this light that he addresses himself to two issues that directly touch upon women: prophesying and praying with uncovered heads (11:2-16) and being disruptive in public services (14:34-35). Because the second embodies a specific command for women to keep silent in the church, we will defer that to our next chapter where we analyze, in some detail, the two Pauline texts invariably cited by those who forbid women to preach or exercise any sort of leadership in the church.

The problem addressed here is that women—so long denied any participation whatsoever in religious worship—were taking their newfound freedom in Christ too far for their culture. Because women were warmly welcomed into the church and encouraged to participate fully in the services (v. 5), they saw no reason to be shackled by the oppressive conventions of a non-Christian culture. Therefore, when they came to church they took off their hats and removed their veils, both despised symbols of their inferior status. For them, it was like casting off chains. They could now worship the living God with no covering over them except the grace of God. Likewise, with **"unveiled face** [they could behold] as in a mirror the glory of the Lord" (2 Cor. 3:18, NASB, emphasis added). What liberation! What innovation! Not since the days when Miriam the prophetess, Moses' sister, took the timbrel in hand and led the Israelite women in singing and dancing following the Exodus event had women enjoyed such freedom in worship (Exod. 15:19-21).

Unfortunately, by flaunting their freedom from standards of social decorum and dress of the day, Christian women had become an embarrassment in the church and a scandal outside. Immediately preceding this passage, Paul argues that "'all things are lawful,' but not all things are beneficial. 'All things are lawful,' but not all things build up" (10:23). He follows that up by enunciating, once again, the basic law of love, which ought to guide all social relations, especially those in the church: "Do not seek your own advantage, but that of the other" (v. 24).

From that base, he makes his appeal to women by saying, "But I want you to understand that Christ is the head of every man, and the husband is the head of his wife, and God is the head of Christ" (11:3). As we shall see when we analyze Eph. 5:23, headship does not imply a wooden hierarchy in the Body of Christ but implies a dynamic principle of love based upon the voluntary subordination of one's rights on behalf of congregational order. If Paul meant to convey a hierarchical order moving from superior to inferior in 11:3, then he would have listed God as the "head of Christ" first instead of last.

What is striking about this passage, however, is that women are "praying and prophesying" (NASB) in the church at Corinth right alongside men (11:4-5). **There were women preachers in the church at Corinth.** Prophecy, in the Scriptures, has more to do with forthtelling than fore-telling. A prophet was one who possessed a "gifted faculty for setting forth divinely revealed truth."[6] The church at Corinth enjoyed all the benefits of being led in prayer not only by men but by women. They had the advantage of hearing God's Word declared from not only a masculine but a feminine perspective as well. This rare and wonder-ful privilege has, unfortunately, been denied to most Chris-tians, due to a tragic misunderstanding of Paul's intent in his special instructions directed to a specific problem situa-tion (see the next chapter). Paul obviously has no interest in silencing women in Corinth but only in making sure that those who pray or prophesy will do so in a manner that will not detract from the public ministry of the Word.

His argument runs along two lines. First, he appeals to social convention: "Does not even nature itself teach you that if a man has long hair, it is a dishonor to him, but if a woman has long hair, it is a glory to her? For her hair is given to her for a covering" (11:14-15, NASB). By uncover-ing their heads women ran the risk of being mistaken for the cult prostitutes of Corinth who went about in public not only with heads uncovered but with hair cut close or even shaved (v. 6). Second, he makes a theological argu-ment. When he says that man "is the image and glory of God; but the woman is the glory of man" (v. 7, NASB), he is not rewriting Gen. 1:26-27 where the woman shares equally with the man in bearing and exhibiting God's im-age. John Bristow argues that Paul is referring, rather, to the way Jews worshiped.[7] He points out that the Jews wore head coverings during worship, called the tallith, in order to shield themselves from God's Shechinah glory. Since "the glory of God [is now revealed] in the face of Christ" (2 Cor. 4:6, NASB), there is no longer any need for a man to worship with his head covered. "To cover one's head, Paul seems to be saying, is to act as if one were ashamed of Christ, our head, who is the image and glory of God."[8] For the woman, however, a head covering functioned in that culture as a wedding ring in ours: it reflected the "glory" of her husband. To cast it off would be to shame him.

If, then, head covering was associated with the idea of "glory" by the culture of the day, then retention of head covering by the women would convey the blessing of, and the connection to, Christ's glory upon the woman. The symbol of the authority conferred upon her in Christ is demonstrated by the head covering. "Therefore," says Paul, "the woman ought to have a symbol of authority on her head, because of the angels" (11:10, NASB). What "authority"? Some commentators hold that a woman has authority over her own head as to her hair and head coverings. Others think it refers to the "head," her husband (v. 3), in which case the wife would have authority over her husband. Most likely, Paul is saying that a woman ought to respect social convention and wear an acceptable head covering, especially when praying or prophesying in public services.

New Testament specialists are at a loss as to what Paul is referring to when he says, "because of the angels." The second-century Church father, Tertullian, thought that if angels looked down and saw women with heads and faces uncovered, they might fall in love with them. Bristow points out, however, that this may refer to the role that angels played, in the Gospels, in affirming women. Angels were active in announcing Christ's birth to Mary and in proclaiming Christ's resurrection to the women at the tomb. Bristow further notes, "The fact that angels came to women affirms the spiritual authority women may enjoy from God and that they may exercise within the church of Christ."[9]

There is another explanation for Paul's argument throughout this section (11:3-10). Virginia Mollenkott suggests that the apostle is making his appeal for women to dress according to custom by citing the patriarchal "order of creation."[10] Since social customs are not buttressed by timeless truth but vary from culture to culture, he reverts back to his earlier rabbinic training and avers that covered heads and veiled faces are an appropriate way for women to honor an otherwise harmless social convention.

It is of vital importance, however, to note that **Paul challenges and destroys the traditionalist "order of creation" rationale** in the next two verses: "Nevertheless, **in the Lord** woman is not independent of man or man independent of woman. **For just as woman came from man, so man comes through woman;** but all things come from God" (11:11-12, emphasis added). True, the first woman originated from the man. Lest prideful man be tempted to lord it over the woman—as indeed has been the case—God ordained that after the first Adam, every man would originate from a woman. So much for male superiority because of being first in creation!

Once again, it is important to keep the overall picture in mind. Paul's objective here is not to analyze male-female relationships but to encourage sensitivity, on the part of women, to the sensibilities of others regarding appropriate dress and behavior in public worship, particularly when praying and prophesying before the whole congregation.

Paul deals extensively with the exercise of spiritual gifts in the church (chap. 12). While he does not specifically mention women, he does use such qualifiers as "each one" and "all persons" without distinction between men and women. Likewise, he affirms that all the Corinthians were "baptized into one body—Jews or Greeks, slaves or free ["male and female"—Gal. 3:28]—and we were all made to drink of one Spirit" (v. 13). We can assume, therefore, that he encourages women, as well as men, to exercise their God-given spiritual gifts "for the common good" (v. 7). Perhaps Paul had women especially in mind, given the cultural bias against them, when he observes,

> The members of the body that seem to be weaker are indispensable, and those members of the body that we think less honorable we clothe with greater honor, and our less respectable members are treated with greater respect; whereas our more respectable members do not need this. But God has so arranged the body, giving the greater honor to the inferior member, that there may be no dissension within the body, but the members may have the same care for one another (*vv.* 22-25).

Paul would have been appalled at the discrimination that has dominated the church since then, splitting the Body of Christ asunder along gender lines, artificially limiting women's range of expression when it comes to their God-given, Spirit-incited gifts. **To withhold certain offices and functions from women institutionalizes divisiveness in the Body based on no higher principle than that of physical gender!**

GALATIANS

Paul's explosive letter to the Galatians, believed to be his first, sets out his gospel of reconciliation and emancipation in Christ: "There is no longer Jew or Greek, there is no longer slave or free, there is no longer male and female; for all of you are one in Christ Jesus" (Gal. 3:28). This enunciates his lofty vision of a once-divided world at last united in Christ. Paul sets the stage for this great proclamation when, in 3:10-14, he says that to be an adopted child of God means to be released from the "curse of the law" (v. 13). Through a woman came the curse that bound all of her children—particularly her daughters—under the bondage of discriminatory laws. Likewise, through a woman came Christ who "redeemed us from the curse of the law" (v. 13). He continues this nontraditional truth in the next chapter when he affirms, "But when the fullness of time had come, God sent his Son, born of a woman, born under the law, in order to redeem those who were under the law, so that we might receive adoption as children" (4:4-5).

Under the Law only men could receive their father's inheritance. Now in Christ women, as well as men, become full partakers of the inheritance that belongs to all of Abraham's spiritual children (3:15-29; 4:7). Under the old dispensation, sons were more highly valued than daughters. In the new, all are children of God, and all share equally as members of His family (3:23-26). Formerly, only Jewish males were considered to be true Israelites and bore in their flesh the identifying mark of circumcision. But now, all believers—Jew and Gentile, bond and free, male and female—share one baptism into one body in Christ (vv. 6-14, 27-29): "For in Christ Jesus neither circumcision nor uncircumcision means anything, but faith working through love" (5:6, NASB). The clothes that signified Adam and Eve's alienation from each other have now been replaced by new garments of reconciliation, for we are all "clothed . . . with Christ" (3:27).

To illustrate the freedom we have in Christ, Paul contrasts two covenants: Hagar who represents those "born according to the flesh," and Sarah who represents those born "through the promise" (4:23). What is astonishing about Paul's allegory is that he uses two women, Hagar and Sarah, instead of their two sons, Ishmael and Isaac, as contrasting models. In doing so, he was, once again, breaking with rabbinic tradition. In deliberately accenting Hagar and Sarah, Paul was showing that women were more than bit players in the drama of salvation history: they were prime actors. God is no respecter of persons or gender.

Not surprisingly, given the long and unquestioned acceptance of patriarchy and social hierarchies, many voices have been raised to blunt the full force of Paul's radical proclamation. In an effort to remove the apparent contradiction between Gal. 3:28 and other passages where Paul specifically prohibits women from speaking or teaching in church, traditionalists hold to a "spiritual interpretation"; that is, Paul is referring to our standing "in Christ" and not our standing in church or society. They maintain that Gal. 3:28 constitutes a soteriological statement that has nothing to do with social issues, nor does it change positions and roles assigned in creation. Others affirm that the equality envisioned here by Paul awaits the *eschaton;* that is, it describes the "age that is to come." Others, such as the Evangelicals who framed the "Danvers Statement," maintain that while Paul does enunciate a position of equality in principle, he held to patriarchal hierarchy in practice.

These interpretations that spiritualize away the force of Paul's egalitarian declaration have likewise been used by Christians in defense of slavery as a divinely ordained social institution. They, too, admitted that Paul destroys slavery in principle in Gal. 3:28 as well as in his letter to Philemon (vv. 10-17), yet they maintained that he encouraged Christians to accommodate themselves to it in practice (Col. 3:2—4:1).

Klyne Snodgrass asserts, however, that "Galatians 3:26-29 functions as the climax of the epistle." He states: "Paul's point is that faith in Christ has brought a new status (children of God) and a new existence (incorporation into Christ). . . . The parallel structure found in 3:26 and 3:28 emphasizes that all have the same status as children of God and that all enjoy the unity that is in Christ."[11] He concludes his exhaustive study of this text by stating that

"Galatians 3:28 prohibits the valuations and divisions of the old order and insists on equal standing and unity in Christ."[12] Don Williams agrees:

> Male dominance, egotism, patriarchal power and preferential priority is at an end. No longer can Genesis 2-3 be employed to reduce woman to an inferior position or state. If redemption is real the warfare between the sexes is over. At the same time, female seduction, manipulation, and domineering is also over, "for you are all one in Christ Jesus."
>
> Furthermore, the life-style of the church must be consistent with the gospel of the church. Proclamation must result in demonstration. . . . We conclude that the old barriers are broken as Christ makes all things new.[13]

Gal. 3:28 became the Magna Charta text for Evangelicals advocating the abolition of slavery, as well as the enfranchisement of women. Gilbert Haven, early 19th-century Methodist bishop, called this verse Paul's "greatest doctrine of Woman's Rights."[14] Antoinette Brown, in 1850, became the first woman preacher to be ordained in American history, and one of the first since the earliest centuries of the Church. Luther Lee, who preached at her ordination service, used Gal. 3:28 as his text. He declared:

> In the Church of which Christ is the only head, males and females possess equal rights and privileges. . . . To make any distinction in the church of Jesus Christ, between males and females, purely on the ground of sex is virtually to strike this text from the sacred volume, for it affirms that in Christ there is no difference between males and females, that they are all one in regard to the gospel of the grace of God.[15]

One year after the first women's rights convention in 1848, Elizabeth Wilson wrote *A Scriptural View of Woman's Rights and Duties*, in which she made these comments upon this text: "There are no exclusively privileged classes among Christ's disciples—no monopolists—not only is there no distinction of eternal salvation between male and female . . . but they have the same rights and privileges."[16] Susie Stanley, evangelical scholar and biblical feminist, concludes: "I have found this text to be a rallying cry in the movement for women's rights and the recovery of the New Testament practice of women in ministry. . . . this text has been a biblical verification of the calling to ministry that women have experienced through the Holy Spirit. We in evangelical churches should affirm the equality in ministry advocated in Galatians 3:28."[17]

EPHESIANS

Paul's letter to the Ephesians is centered around the conviction that all things are moving to their final consummation in Christ (1:9-10). Sin deadens; Christ makes alive (2:1-7). Sin excludes; Christ includes (vv. 11-13). Sin erects dividing walls; Christ tears them down (vv. 14-15). Sin alienates; Christ reconciles (vv. 16-18). Sin estranges; Christ embraces (v. 19—3:12).

It is in this context that Paul offers one of the most exalted and liberating expositions ever committed to writing concerning how husbands and wives ought to relate together (5:21-33). What is so distressing, however, is to see the way in which the beauty of Paul's magnificent vision and the radicality of his revelation about "kingdom relationships" has all but been lost because of the extraordinary attention focused upon only one side of the relationship: "Wives, be subject to your own husbands, as to the Lord" (5:22, NASB; cf. Col. 3:18). The breadth and range of his insight into the possibilities for Christian marriage, patterned after Christ's love for His bride, the Church, has been skewered upon the altars of biased and truncated hierarchical interpretations that totally distort what Paul is trying to communicate. Actually, if commanding women to be in subjection to their husbands was all he had to say, he might as well have saved his breath. There was nothing new or particularly spiritual in that.

Likewise, there is no shortage of voices today calling for a return to "traditional family values" where women are bound under an ironclad subordination to their husbands. They are advocating women to abandon their freedom in Christ to become "subject again to a yoke of slavery" (Gal. 5:1, NASB). Helen Andelin's *Fascinating Womanhood* and Marabel Morgan's enormously popular *The Total Woman* were but the leading edge of a tidal wave of "submissionism" literature that has poured forth from the bosom of evangelical Christianity in recent decades. Both authors unquestioningly accept the patriarchal order of dominant male and docile female as representing a divinely ordained hierarchy, and they support their case by appealing to one narrow part of Paul's teaching while ignoring the rest. They teach not only that the husband is superior by divine decree, but that it is the wife's God-given responsibility to massage his feelings of masculinity, aggressiveness, and dominance. Thus Andelin exhorts the ideal woman "to become the fragile dependent creature that nature intended you to be."[18]

Marabel Morgan goes a giant step further by encouraging a wife to adore her husband: "It is only when a woman surrenders her life to her husband, reveres and worships him, and is willing to serve him, that she becomes really beautiful to him."[19] Such language smacks of idolatry. The sad lesson of history is that when a woman worships a man as a god, he does not become more divine but more beastly, even demonic. And the woman does not become more beautiful but less human, in her own eyes as well as in his.

If we are to be "rightly dividing the word of truth" (2 Tim. 2:15, KJV), we must set Paul's special teaching about marital relationships within the larger context of unity in Christ. It is impossible to imagine that in a letter celebrating the breaking down of dividing walls and the bridging of chasms in Christ, Paul would suddenly reverse himself and interject a dominance-subordination division into the very heart of the most basic and important of all human relationships, that between husband and wife. It is hard to believe that the apostle who celebrated "everything has become new" in Christ (2 Cor. 5:17) would revert back to defending a pattern of ruler-ruled relationships that had plagued humankind since the Fall.

To restore perspective to Paul's profound and radically innovative teaching concerning husband-wife relationships, we must draw the larger picture. After proclaiming the great theological truth of unity in Christ (Ephesians 1—3), Paul begins to show how it works out in practical life (4—6). He begins this section by saying: "I therefore, the prisoner in the Lord, beg you to lead a life worthy of the calling to which you have been called" (4:1). What are the controlling principles in such a "worthy walk"? "Humility and gentleness, with patience, bearing with one another in love, making every effort to maintain the unity of the Spirit in the bond of peace" (vv. 2-3). It is hard to imagine how these qualities of spirit would work in a patriarchal model, particularly on the part of the one ordained to rule.

Paul repeats this principle of self-giving love when he says, "Therefore be imitators of God, as beloved children, and live in love, as Christ loved us" (5:1-2a). And how does Christ express His love for us? He "gave himself up for us, a fragrant offering and sacrifice to God" (v. 2b). After showing how self-giving love applies to a number of ethical and moral issues, Paul concludes this section by encouraging us to "be subject to one another out of reverence for Christ" (v. 21). If we love with Christ's kind of love, then it follows that we will, like Him, offer up ourselves to one another in love (cf. 4:32).

Having enunciated the principle of self-giving love and applied it to specific situations, Paul is now ready to show how it ought to work between husbands and wives. He begins by repeating only what many had said before him: "Wives, be subject to your husbands as you are to the Lord" (5:22). The picture that this verse conjures in our minds is that of a king sitting upon his throne with his subjects groveling before him in abject and unquestioning obedience.

There is, however, a startling omission in the Greek text that is not apparent in English: "be subject to" does not even appear in verse 22! The text literally reads, "Wives to their husbands as to the Lord." Wives are to do what to their husbands? To make grammatical sense, translators have pulled down the verb "be subject to" from the preceding verse: "be subject to one another in the fear of Christ" (v. 21, NASB). What is requested of wives is exactly that required of all believers in the Body of Christ: participation in voluntary mutual submission (vv. 18-20). The kind of subjection called for here has nothing to do with subservience and obedience but everything to do with a humble spirit of self-giving love. John Bristow is right on target when he points out that "it would be as impossible for a group of people to be obedient to each other as it would be for a group to follow each other."[20]

There is a Greek word that can be translated "be subject to" that means "be obedient unto": it is *hupakouo*, often used to describe master-slave and parent-child relationships. It is the word Paul uses when he writes in the next chapter, "Children, obey [*hupakouo*] your parents in the Lord" (6:1). This is the word that both Greek philosophers and rabbis used to describe husband-wife relationships.

Not so Paul. When referring to the quality of relationships that ought to prevail within the body of believers and in Christian marriages, he used another word, *hupotasso*. In its active form it does describe the relationship between a conqueror and the vanquished as when the disciples, returning from their preaching mission, reported that "even the demons **are subject to** us" (Luke 10:17, NASB, emphasis added). But Paul never uses this word in its active form to describe human relationships. He does not order believers—much less husbands—to "dominate" or "vanquish" one another. Instead he uses the imperative middle voice form, *hupotassomai*, which suggests a voluntary submission. As we have already noted, "be subject to" in verse 21 cannot mean that believers are to obey one another but rather ought to cooperate with one another.

From our study of both the Greek word and the context in which it is used, we need to translate "be subject to" as "be sensitive to," "be supportive of," "be loyal to," "be responsive to," or as the German translation renders *hupotassomai*, "place yourself at the disposition of one another."[21] Subjection has nothing to do with a position of inferiority or powerlessness but has everything to do with spiritual powerfulness; that is, it demonstrates personal self-esteem and strength of character in deliberately choosing to humble oneself on behalf of the beloved, or to "one another" in the Body of Christ.

The next verses seem to support female submissionism: "For the husband is the head of the wife just as Christ is the head of the church, the body of which he is the Savior. Just as the church is subject to Christ, so also wives ought to be, in everything, to their husbands" (5:23-24). When we read "head" in our English translations, we immediately assume that this implies leadership, decision making, and authority, as in head of state. The analogy seems clear; even as the head (husband) directs the body, so the body (wife) obediently submits to the head.

Before we leap to this conclusion, however, we need to recognize, as Virginia Mollenkott points out, that the connection between the physical head and the body through the nervous system was not known in biblical times. To the contrary, "decision-making was located in the *heart*, which is why we are told that our belief in Jesus is to take place in our hearts, and that thoughts issue from the heart (Romans 10:9; Matthew 15:19; Hebrews 4:12; and so forth)."[22]

We see this most clearly when we note the Greek word Paul selected for "head." If Paul wanted to convey a master-slave or king-subject relationship, he would have used the Greek word *arche*, which is translated "beginning," or "first things" as in *archaeology, archetype, architect*. It also means "of first in importance," as in *archangel, archbishop, archenemy*. This word appears numerous times in the New Testament, including Paul's letters, to designate leadership and authority, such as "magistrate," "chief," "prince," "ruler," "principalities," "authorities," and "head." So if Paul intended to describe the relationship between God and Christ, Christ and man, man and woman in a pattern of hierarchical authority, a "chain of command," he would have used the word *arche*, as Aristotle did when describing the relationship between husband and wife. There are 46 Greek words that Paul could have chosen to speak of Kingdom relationships that would have conveyed the idea of rank and position, but he did not.

Instead, Paul deliberately selected another Greek word, *kephale*, which, even though it is sometimes used to describe the head as a part of one's body, it was never used to mean chief, or boss, or ruler, or authority.[23] *Kephale* most often means "source" or "origination of life" as in 1 Cor. 11:8, "For man does not originate from woman, but woman from man" (NASB). This is in reference to Genesis 2 where man is formed first and then the woman. Man, however, has his source in Christ, and Christ has His source in

God (Col. 1:15-18). Paul defines what he means by "head" in Col. 1:18 when he says, "He is the head *[kephale]* of the body, the church; he is the beginning, the firstborn from the dead, so that he might come to have first place in everything."

Christ's headship over the Church does not derive from the "divine right of kings" or some sort of preordained hierarchy but by virtue of being at once the Church's Source (beginning, first cause) and Reconciler (Savior, Redeemer). Headship, therefore, does not suggest an externally imposed authority or rulership but rather suggests resource, enabler, and advocate. Headship is servant-leadership that springs from self-giving love (Col. 1:19-21). This is further seen when Paul urges Christians to hold fast "to the head *[kephale],* from whom the whole body, nourished and held together by its ligaments and sinews, grows with a growth that is from God" (2:19). Christ's Lordship is not organizational as God's chief executive officer but organic and dynamic as a vine that gives life to the branches (John 15:1-13). The life Christ gives to "the whole body" derives from His willingness to "lay down his life for his friends" (John 15:13, NASB).

Precisely, how does Christ exercise His headship over the Church, and thus the husband exercise his headship over his wife? Paul's answer is, "Christ **loved** the church and **gave himself up for her**" (5:25, emphasis added). The authority that Christ exercises over His Church as its head is not like that of the Gentiles. To the contrary, **it is the authority of servant-leadership exercised in the power of self-giving love.** "For the Son of Man came not to be served but to serve, and to give his life a ransom for many" (Mark 10:45). In other words, **Christ turns the world's (Gentile's) understanding of** *arche* **headship right on its head.** He speaks not of *arche*-ship (rulership) but of *kephale*-ship (servanthood) and in doing so destroys the fundamental assumptions of patriarchalism as well as all externally imposed social hierarchies within the Body of Christ.

The phrase "chain of command," frequently used to describe a gender-ordered hierarchy of social relationships, is a most inappropriate metaphor. "Chain" suggests bondage and oppression. "Command" implies the rule of law and the external imposition of power. While such concepts accurately describe the way husbands and wives related to each other under the curse of sin (Gen. 3:16), they are totally incompatible with the "reign of grace" instituted by Christ Jesus our Lord. So, when we confront words like "headship" and "authority" in the New Testament, we must take into consideration the radically new content Christ pours into them.

Paul follows up his specific counsel to wives by an innovative and radically surprising command directed to husbands: "Husbands, **love your wives,** just as Christ loved the church and gave himself up for her. . . . In the same way, **husbands should love their wives** as they do their own bodies. He who loves his wife loves himself" (Eph. 5:25, 28, emphasis added). When Paul instructed, "Wives, [be subject] to your own husbands" (v. 22, NASB), he was not saying anything new. However, when he commanded, "Husbands, love your wives," he was voicing words never heard before. Neither in the Old Testament nor in the Talmud—the massive compilation of Jewish rabbinical teachings across the centuries—nor in any Gentile literature of the biblical era is there anything comparable to this. None of the great founders of other world religions ever said anything like that. The law of Moses commanded, "You shall love your neighbor as yourself" (Lev. 19:18), but nowhere specified that a husband should love his wife. The Talmud laid upon the husband the obligation to provide and care for his wife and not mistreat her, but it falls short of encouraging him to love her. Likewise, it is rare to read in antiquity where any man, within or outside biblical tradition, professed love for his wife. A man might declare his love for Caesar, or his best friend, or his mistress, or his horse, but love his wife? Why would he do that?[24]

Paul's counsel to husbands is even more striking when we note the word he used for "love." He avoided *eros*, which describes physical attraction, and *phileo*, which speaks of friendship, and the affection one has for his family or tribe or country. Rather, Paul deliberately chose a word that appears only rarely outside the New Testament, a word into which Jesus and the early Christians poured an entirely new meaning: *agape*. Its definition was formed and filled out by the sacrifice of Christ on the Cross. It came to mean "self-sacrificing, self-giving love." It is the word Paul used when he wrote, "But God proves his love *[agape]* for us in that while we still were sinners Christ died for us" (Rom. 5:8). Likewise John when he said, "In this is love *[agape]*, not that we loved God but that he loved us and sent his Son to be the atoning sacrifice for our sins" (1 John 4:10).

The leadership that a husband exercises on behalf of his wife, then, has nothing to do with commanding or demanding but everything to do with giving and sacrificing. The dynamic principle governing husband-wife relationships, modeled after Christ's love for the Church, is not a power-driven hierarchy but a self-giving attitude of **mutual submission.** Each submits to the other and serves the other, as both submit to and serve Christ who in turn exercises His headship over the Church by giving up His life for her sake.

Once again, Paul goes against the chauvinist grain of his heritage and culture. By making sure that there will be no justification for a husband lording it over his wife, he reaffirms the truth revealed in the original creation story: namely, **women have infinite worth as bearers of the im-**

age of God himself. They ought to be loved for their own sakes with the same kind of self-giving love by which Christ loves His Church! The only hierarchy that fits within Kingdom relationships is where the first continually seek to be the last and the least. It is the posture, not of a king but of a servant. It is Calvary love: the kind of *agape* love reflected in Jesus' Gethsemane prayer, "Not as I will, but as thou wilt" (Matt. 26:39, KJV). Husbands and wives, men and women are to live together—not under the rule of law but within the reign of grace. The proper paradigm for relating to one another "in Christ" is not that of a king sitting high upon his throne but that of a servant bowed low with a towel about his waist and a wash basin in his hands.

This is only a partial survey of all that Paul has to say about women. Yet if we were to examine the rest of his writings—excluding the two difficult passages that are the special focus of the next chapter—they would be consistent with what we have discovered to this point. We can summarize the apostle's position regarding women as follows: First, men and women are created equally in the image and glory of God, share equally in the curse of sin, and participate equally in the grace of redemption. Second, marriage relationships are not to be ordered according to an externally imposed hierarchy "according to the law" but by an internally embraced expression of self-giving love through **mutual submission and full partnership.** Third, women have just as much right as men to exercise their spiritual gifts in the Church and fulfill their ministry, especially if they are called to preach. The wholeness and the health of the Church depends upon the freedom of each individual to exercise his or her spiritual gift and calling to the fullest.

·6

Texts Prohibiting
the Public Ministry
of Women

*W*e come now to the two passages that, more than any other biblical texts, have been used to justify institutional discrimination against women in the church. On the basis of these prohibitions, women, who have comprised the greater part of the Church across the centuries, have been denied entrance into the sanctum sanctorum of ministerial leadership. Furthermore, for Spirit-filled women themselves, the use made of these texts has snuffed out any stirring they might have felt in terms of a call to preach, or the exercise of their spiritual gifts in public ministry. The Church has been immeasurably weakened, having been deprived of the potential contribution that gifted women might otherwise have made. In short, the interpretations of these texts have done more mischief than any others in the entire New Testament. And it has all been so unnecessary.

The tragedy is that these passages have been ripped out of context with no regard for the unique situations represented in the churches at Corinth and Ephesus, and thus have been distorted in their meaning and perverted in their intention. Nothing is more important for us, if we would do justice to the apostle Paul, than "handling accurately the word of truth" (2 Tim. 2:15, NASB). Let us turn our attention now to a close analysis of each troubling passage.

THE QUESTION OF SILENCE

> Let the women keep silent in the churches; for they are not permitted to speak, but let them subject themselves, just as the Law also says. And if they desire to learn anything, let them ask their own husbands at home; for it is improper for a woman to speak in church (1 Cor. 14:34-35, NASB).

These verses appear, at first reading, to contradict everything that Paul has taught and practiced to this point. How can he acknowledge women praying and prophesying in public worship without one word of prohibition or condemnation in chapter 11 and then command them to keep silent in chapter 14? How were the women who worked alongside him as *diakonos*—fellow ministers whom he so warmly commends in Romans 16, as well as in other places—to exercise their ministry in the church if such a gag rule were in place? Is he, in this instance, capitulating to social convention and entrenched patriarchal tradition, thus falling under his own indictment of the Galatians when he asked, "Having begun by the Spirit, are you now being perfected by the flesh?" (3:3, NASB).

Adding to our difficulty is the rationale given in this passage for silencing women: "just as the Law also says." What law? None in the Old Testament. To the contrary, the laws of Moses were noteworthy for their egalitarian application; that is, they applied to rich and poor, bond and free, and men and women alike. The "Law" here mentioned refers rather to the Talmudic "Traditions of the Elders," which, as we have already seen, forbade women from participation in all public gatherings.

How, then, do we reconcile 1 Cor. 14:34-35 with the advent of the age of the Spirit in which women as well as men have the freedom to preach? (Acts 2:16-18). Furthermore, how do we harmonize this restrictive directive with the even-handed way Paul treats men and women in all the other passages we have surveyed to this point? We answer: with great difficulty.

Scholars and biblical interpreters have struggled with these questions for generations. Some dismiss the problem altogether by asserting that these verses were not written by Paul but represent later interpolations by copyists.[1] There is some textual support for this position in that the Bezan codex (D) and related early Western Greek manuscripts place verses 34-35 at the end of the chapter. This suggests that these verses may have originated as a copyist's "editorializing" that was eventually incorporated into the text itself in different places.[2] This argument has some merit in that these two verses appear to be an interruption to the flow of the passage. They do not fit in the immediate context. They intrude, as it were, "off the wall." They do reflect, however, a later ecclesiology in which male dominance had reasserted itself quite forcefully in the Church.

It is risky, however, to simply strike out disagreeable passages on the basis of textual evidence alone. Likewise, we must reject all attempts to superimpose a wooden consistency upon the Scriptures by such artificial devises, lest the integrity and trustworthiness of God's Word be undermined. In any case, this passage is part of the received canon of sacred Scriptures that the Church holds as authoritative in all matters relating to faith and practice. And it must be dealt with.

Most New Testament commentators before the 1960s agree with Clarence T. Craig, who writes the exegesis of this passage in *The Interpreter's Bible,* "There is no question but that Paul believed in the definite subordination of women (Col. 3:18) and was convinced that the emancipation of women . . . would be a violation of the divine order."[3] The question must be asked, however, whether this interpretation is an unbiased one or whether it emerges from unexamined patriarchal presuppositions. Today many are looking at the old texts more carefully, trying to let them speak for themselves in their first-century context. Their research has brought about some strikingly fresh insights that can only be described as revolutionary. Liberated from a religious and cultural bias against women, New Testament scholars have begun to see that there are nondiscriminatory ways to interpret these passages. Let us see what they are discovering.

R. K. McGregor Wright interprets this passage (1 Cor. 14:34-35) in a novel way. He holds that Paul is exposing and opposing certain men in the Corinthian church who are seeking to bar women from participation in public worship. Paul often states an opponent's position before destroying it (see Rom. 6:1ff.). In this case he first quotes them and their traditionalist rationale in 14:34-35. Then he repudiates their harsh limitation in the next verse (v. 36) by asking, in effect, "What? Was it only from you men that the word of God first went forth? Or has it come to you only?" This rhetorical question can only be answered: "Of course not!"[4] While Wright's solution removes the contradiction in Paul's attitude toward women in ministry, it suffers from a common interpretive trap called eisegesis; that is, he reads more into the text than the context warrants. Furthermore, his interpretation won't work at all when applied to the parallel passage in 1 Tim. 2:11-15.

The weight of textual, contextual, and historical evidence suggests that these verses do represent Paul's attempt to deal with a unique set of problems that were threatening to discredit the gospel and destroy the church at Corinth. So it is of vital importance that we try to understand what was going on, both in the city of Corinth and in the church, if we are to make sense of these verses.

Our problem in interpreting such a passage is much like that of listening in on a telephone conversation. We have access to only half of the dialogue. We can only surmise what the party on the other end is saying by analyzing the response of the one to whom we are listening. This is our dilemma when we read Paul's letters. We can hear, loud and clear, his answers, but we have to reconstruct the questions. We can see his response to problems, but we are often at a loss to understand the underlying issues. Added to our interpretive challenge is that the church at Corinth was like no church we have known. There was no building, no pastor, no constitution or church government, no long-standing tradition, not even any Gospels since they had not yet been written, and certainly no New Testament such as we have. All they had as worship resources were a scroll or two of the Hebrew Scriptures and an earlier letter from Paul that we no longer possess (see 1 Cor. 5:11).

Furthermore, the city of Corinth was like no other we have ever seen. Far from being a secular city, it overflowed with all sorts of exotic religions, including the worship of Aphrodite, the goddess of love, in whose service were some 1,000 cult prostitutes. Of particular interest to us was another well-developed and enormously popular religion devoted to the worship of Bacchus, also known as Dionysus, who is variously described as the "god of wine," the "god of dance," and the "god of madness."[5] One tradition claimed that Bacchus turned water into wine at his annual festival.

Women, especially, were attracted to the Dionysian cult because they found in its exuberant worship complete freedom to express themselves fully in a way denied them by repressive conventional society. Consequently, they went wild. Numerous descriptions from antiquity have survived that describe women, loosened by wine, caught up in religious ecstasy. They engaged in spirited sensuous dancing, accompanied by flutes, cymbals, and drums, sometimes stripping naked. They would shout and speak in unintelligible languages, the "tongues of Bacchus" according to Aristophanes. Such unintelligible speech, uttered at the height of frenetic motion and emotion, was well-known throughout the ancient world. Inscriptions survive that refer to religious women's chanting and shrill cries. Their religious ecstasy sometimes spilled over into sexual promiscuity. Devotees of Bacchus, both men and women, believed it was only when they were "out of their minds" that the soul was released from the body so that they could then enter into mystic communion with the gods. Even among many pagan Corinthians such religious behavior was regarded as outrageous.

Paul asked the Corinthians, "If, therefore, the whole church comes together and all speak in tongues, and outsiders or unbelievers enter, will they not say that you are out of your mind?" (14:23). Many would have responded, "Yes, and we would have it no other way." That was all they knew, coming so recently from their kind of pagan religious background. Hence the gospel of Jesus Christ, which is mediated principally through the Word—words intelligibly spoken and clearly understood—was in danger of being lost in the noise of exuberant worship and the confusion of ecstatic utterances.

Paul's overall purpose, in chapter 14, is to bring some semblance of order into the church (v. 40) so that believers might be edified (vv. 1-4) and so that unbelievers might be converted (v. 25). His rationale is grounded in a theological conviction that "God is not a God of confusion but of peace" (v. 33, NASB). This must have been quite a revelation, given the way they were accustomed to thinking about their gods. While not prohibiting glossolalia (unintelligible speech) outright, verse 1 sets the agenda for the first half of the chapter (vv. 1-25): "Pursue love and strive for the spiritual gifts, and **especially** that you may prophesy" (v. 1, emphasis added). In the second section (vv. 27-36) he suggests rules ordering their worship. He gives instructions to the glossolalists (vv. 27-28), prophets (vv. 29-33), and wives (vv. 34-36). He concludes with a fervent appeal for everything to be "done properly and in an orderly manner" (v. 40, NASB).

"Let **the** women keep silent in the churches" (v. 34, NASB, emphasis added). The use of the definite article in the Greek focuses attention upon a specific group of women, not **all** women. Which women? Those who, through exuberant and chaotic speech, were creating confusion and disorder in the services. From verse 35 we see that Paul's instruction was directed to married women.

There were several words that Paul could have chosen for "silence."[6] One was *phimoo*, which means "to muzzle, tie shut." Jesus used it as a command to quiet the unclean spirit (Mark 1:25). Another word for silence is *hesuchia*, signifying "stillness and quietness." Paul uses this word in 1 Tim. 2:11 when advising women how to study. But he did not use it here. Instead, Paul selected the Greek verb *sigao*, which means a "voluntary silence." It was used to describe Jesus' silence when He stood before Pilate (Mark 14:61) and the silence of the apostles and elders at the Jerusalem Council as Paul and Barnabas reported the reception the gospel received among the Gentiles (Acts 15:12). It is the same word that Paul addresses to men in 1 Cor. 14:28, "let **him** keep silent in the church" (NASB, emphasis added). If both commands are taken out of context and generalized for the whole church at all times, then we would have a church of Trappist monks where everyone is silent all the time! Such blanket silence, however, can hardly be Paul's intention for either men or women.

What about his double command for women not to speak, in both verses 34 and 35? There are many Greek words that can be translated "speak." Five denote a special kind of speaking like preaching, and 25 others can be translated as simply "speak," "say," or "teach." He did not forbid women to preach, teach, pray, sing, or testify in public worship. Instead, he wrote that women are not to *laleo*, which has a broad range of meanings. It can mean both intelligible speech (v. 3) or unintelligible tongues (v. 4). But of all the verbs translated as "speak," only *laleo* can mean simply "talk" or "chatter." Paul is not prohibiting "praying or prophesying" (11:5, NASB) but is prohibiting noisy, idle conversation during the worship service, "for it is improper for a woman to speak [converse, talk] in church" (v. 35, NASB).

Why was this instruction directed primarily to married women? Because in Greek society, as in Jewish, women were shut up in their homes most of the time and had no opportunity to socialize. So when they found such a warm welcome within these newly formed Christian communities, they were drawn out and encouraged to participate and socialize. The net result was noise and confusion, which made an intelligible and ordered worship service an impossibility. It is also likely that, given their Dionysian past, the women in the congregation were given to more extreme expression of glossolalia than were the men.

He follows up by telling them to "subject themselves" (NASB), which has incorrectly been assumed to be yet another submissionism text addressed to wives (Eph. 5:22; Col. 3:18). The male traditionalist bias of the King James Version translators comes brazenly through when they render it "for it is not permitted unto them to speak; but they are commanded to be under obedience." *Hupotassomai* means nothing of the sort. It is exactly the same word Paul uses two verses earlier when he writes, "and the spirits of prophets are subject to prophets" (v. 32, KJV). And it is the same word Paul uses when he counsels all the believers, male and female, to "be subject to one another in the fear of Christ" (Eph. 5:21, NASB). One can hardly be obedient to every member in a congregation! *Hupotassomai* means a voluntary submission of one's rights. In this case Paul is asking women to restrain themselves for the sake of an ordered worship service.

The next phrase reads, "as the law also says." What law? *Nomos*, the Greek word for law, is used in a variety of ways in the New Testament, such as the "law of Moses," the "law of God," the "law of sin and of death," the "law of the Spirit of life," and the "law . . . in my members." The Jews often referred to rabbinic tradition as "the law." The "law" simply means those general principles that apply in a given situation. So verse 34 can be paraphrased in this way: "Let **the** women voluntarily cease from idle chatter and noisy conversation and maintain a reverent attentiveness during worship, as 'the law' of common courtesy and social convention dictates."

In the next verse, Paul appends a further restriction: "And if they desire to learn anything, let them ask their own husbands at home" (v. 35, NASB). We must recall that most of the women in that time were uneducated, illiterate, and totally ignorant of the Word of God. They had been denied access to any public forum where serious inquiry into great spiritual truth and intellectual ideas were pursued. Even their past experiences of pagan religious ecstasy had not prepared them for this. All one has to do is recall their introduction to college or graduate school to understand what a heady experience it can be to be exposed to new truth and great ideas.

For the first time, believing women in Corinth not only found themselves in a spiritually charged and intellectually stimulating setting but also were welcomed as full and equal participants. Naturally, they were full of questions and felt the freedom to voice them. Thirty years of experience as a teacher of Bible and theology, in church and college, has taught me how quickly spirited discussion can get out of hand, moving from honest inquiry to debate, to pontifical statements, to disputations, to the hubbub of innumerable subgroups, and finally to utter chaos if not checked. That is precisely why the church, in its historical development, moved increasingly away from Paul's Corinthian congregational model of the community of the Spirit or body life (cf. 1 Corinthians 12) where each ministers "for the common good" (v. 7), to a more structured hierarchical service led by select official ministers, while the people—both women and men—were relegated to more passive roles as listeners. Walter Liefeld points to a speech by the elder Cato around 200 B.C. in which there are many parallels to Paul's counsel in this passage. He summarizes it as follows:

> The occasion was the discussion of a law . . . that severely limited women's public appearances and activities. The Roman matrons were demonstrating against this and "could not be kept at home by advice or modesty or their husbands orders." They "dared even to approach and appeal to the consuls." Their actions were considered "shameful." They should not have been "running out into the streets and blocking the roads and speaking to other women's husbands." Cato says he should have said to them, "Could you not have made the same requests, each of your own husband, at home?" The speech continues to oppose women's public appearance and speaking, accusing them of seeking not only liberty but license.[7]

And so, in light of the historical situation in Corinth, we are justified in paraphrasing Paul's intentions (vv. 34-35) in this manner: "True, you women have the freedom to express yourselves fully in the congregation of Christ—and I do want to encourage you to pray publicly and prophesy for the edification of all [11:5; 12:5]. However, for the sake of an ordered church service, restrain yourselves from undue exhibitionism in the exercise of spiritual gifts. Avoid idle conversation once the service has begun, and hold your questions until you can discuss them fully in the privacy of your home with your husband. Be careful to observe accepted social convention in dress and personal decorum in church in order that all may worship in a proper manner and that no unnecessary offense come upon the gospel" (11:5-10).

Seen in this light, Paul was dealing constructively with a local problem situation that ought not to be construed as instituting a universal rule prohibiting women, in perpetuity, from participating actively in worship or from exercising a meaningful ministry.

THE QUESTION OF AUTHORITY

> Let a woman learn in silence with full submission. I permit no woman to teach or to have authority over a man; she is to keep silent. For Adam was formed first, then Eve; and Adam was not deceived, but the woman was deceived and became a transgressor. Yet she will be saved through childbearing, provided they continue in faith and love and holiness, with modesty (1 Tim. 2:11-15).

These verses present even more problems than the Corinthian passage. There is, in verses 11-12, not only a restatement of the injunction against women speaking in church but also a further rule: "I permit no woman to teach or to have authority over a man." Strange that he would make this kind of rule in the church where Priscilla had engaged in such an effective ministry of instructing Apollos concerning the gospel of Jesus Christ (Acts 18:2-3, 18, 24-

28), especially since he also sends them his greetings (2 Tim. 4:19). The rationale given for silencing women is to cite the order of creation (v. 13) by which Jewish males defended female subordination; that is, since man was created first, he has preeminence over women. We have already seen, in our study of 1 Cor. 11:8-12, that Paul rejects this argument out of hand. First, it does not reflect the believing woman's standing "in the Lord." Second, it ignores the fact that, after Adam, God himself reversed the order of creation.

A second reason for enjoining silence upon women is offered in 1 Tim. 2:14, which, again, owes its genesis not to any clear teaching found in either Testament but to rabbinical tradition; that is, since "the woman was deceived and became a transgressor," she cannot be trusted with either teaching offices or leadership roles. If, however, "There is therefore now no condemnation for those who are in Christ Jesus" (Rom. 8:1), why were Christian women required to live under Eve's curse (Gen. 3:16)? Paul himself, however, draws quite the opposite conclusion from the Genesis story of the Fall in his other letters, as we noted previously. He affirms that "just as sin came into the world through one man, and death came through sin, and so death spread to all because all have sinned . . . death exercised dominion from Adam to Moses, even over those whose sins were not like the transgression of Adam" (Rom. 5:12, 14). Adam, rather than Eve, was most responsible for the entrance of sin and death into the world. Eve was deceived but Adam was not. He disobeyed with his eyes wide open. His was a knowing, deliberate, and dispassionate act of sin. Therefore his guilt was the greater.

This restrictive passage concludes with what appears to be a patronizing statement: "But women shall be preserved through the bearing of children if they continue in faith and love and sanctity with self-restraint" (1 Tim. 2:15,

NASB). The implication is that both a woman's salvation and her worth as a human being are dependent upon her biological function as a bearer of children. Where, then, does this leave the single or the barren woman? While this demeaning view was prevalent in Judaism, it is impossible to imagine Jesus expressing such a low estimate of a woman's status before God.

So then, what do we make of this difficult passage that has been used across nearly 2,000 years to deny women their full rights as "fellow citizens with the saints" (Eph. 2:19, NASB), and that so patently contradicts the overwhelming weight of both Jesus' and Paul's teaching elsewhere? Toss them out? Reject them as Holy Scripture? Marcion, an influential second-century Gnostic Christian, did just that. He was the first in church history to propose a canon of sacred Scripture for Christians (ca. A.D. 150). While he included the other 10 letters of Paul, he rejected the Pastorals (1 and 2 Timothy, Titus) simply because he did not believe they came from Paul's hand. He noted, correctly, that they differed radically in style and content from Paul's unquestionably genuine letters.

Many New Testament scholars agree, and they argue persuasively that the Pastoral Epistles do not come directly from the hand of Paul but from "Paulinists," students of Paul in the late first or early second century A.D. One of their grounds for rejecting Pauline authorship is this teaching concerning women that appears to contradict Paul's egalitarian teachings in his other letters. Yet it does reflect a second-century ecclesiology when the church, in its efforts to combat heresies in which women played a conspicuous role, reverted to prohibiting women from teaching or exercising any leadership roles.

While we do admit that linguistically and stylistically there are many differences between the Pastorals and his other letters, we are persuaded that they were written by

Paul, albeit late in his life when his concerns were concentrated more upon preserving the integrity of the gospel than upon its propagation. Writing from prison in Rome, and thus no longer able to directly participate in evangelism and church planting, his attention was now focused upon strengthening his young churches, particularly in "sound doctrine." In any case, we believe the Pastoral Epistles to be inspired ("God-breathed") Holy Scripture and thus must be taken at face value and with utmost seriousness.

The gospel, then as now, did not come into a religious vacuum. As in our discussion of 1 Cor. 14:34-35, we are greatly helped in our understanding of this restrictive passage when we reconstruct the other side of Paul's conversation with Timothy. This church at Ephesus, of which Timothy was the pastoral leader, was born in a storm of conflict and established in the midst of competing pagan religions (Acts 19:1-7, 9, 13-19, 23-41; 20:17-31; 1 Cor. 16:8-9; Eph. 4:14; 5:6-12). We see clearly from reading 1 and 2 Timothy that, a decade later, the church continued to battle with all sorts of

> strange doctrines, . . . myths and endless genealogies . . . mere speculation . . . fruitless discussion . . . blasphem[y] . . . doctrines of demons . . . men who forbid marriage and advocate abstaining from foods . . . worldly fables . . . controversial questions and disputes about words . . . constant friction between men of depraved mind and deprived of the truth, who suppose that godliness is a means of gain . . . men who have gone astray from the truth saying that the resurrection has already taken place . . . those who enter into households and captivate weak women weighed down with sins, led on by various impulses . . . evil people and impostors . . . wanting to have their ears tickled, they will accumulate for themselves teachers in accordance to their own desires; and will turn away their ears

from the truth, and will turn aside to myths (*1 Tim. 1:3-4, 6, 20; 4:1, 3, 7; 6:4-5; 2 Tim. 2:18, 23; 3:6, 13; 4:3-4, NASB*).

The church at Ephesus was, theologically speaking, a "house of horrors!" While the church at Corinth wrestled with moral and ethical problems, the church at Ephesus was plagued by all sorts of strange philosophical mythologies.

Ephesus was a dynamic, diverse, and multicultural seacoast city of enormous prestige and influence. The city offered a smorgasbord of exotic religions, imported from all parts of the world. Included among these were highly unorthodox strains of Jewish teaching ("pay no attention to Jewish myths" [Titus 1:14, NIV]). Even as the disciples and earliest Christians could not escape their Jewish background, with all of its religious limitations and cultural distortions, neither were the Gentile believers able to quickly transcend their pagan presuppositions upon becoming Christians. Consequently, the first generation of Ephesian Christians represented a syncretistic blend of the gospel and all sorts of other religious ideas foreign to the truth as Paul and Timothy preached it in Christ Jesus. Paul understood the problem these new converts were having, for he acknowledged that he was "formerly a blasphemer, a persecutor, and a man of violence. But I received mercy because I had acted ignorantly in unbelief" (1 Tim. 1:13). Paul knew from his own experience that false theology leads to wrong living. Hence the enormous importance he placed upon "sound teaching . . . conforming to godliness" (v. 10; 6:3, NASB).

How, then, does Paul propose to counteract heresy and promote the true faith? His general response to the multiple heresies that troubled the church begins in 1 Tim. 2:1-7, where he urges prayers to be made on behalf of all people to a gracious God "who desires everyone to be saved and to come to the knowledge of the truth" (v. 4).

Why? So that "we may lead a quiet and peaceable life in all godliness and dignity" (v. 2). This was in sharp contrast to the raucous noise of quarrels and conflict that disturbed the peace of the church.

Behind 1 Tim. 2:5-6 lies a particular strain of pagan mythology that is important to note, particularly as we deal with the matter of women preaching. Richard and Catherine Clark Kroeger have made an exhaustive study of the philosophical and religious ideas that dominated the Mediterranean world of that day.[8] Goddess worship, to which women were especially drawn, was prevalent. It worshiped the "female spiritual principle" in deity. Goddesses were also embraced as mediators who enabled devotees to attain a mystic union with the deity, often through sexual intercourse with a sacred prostitute. Even Hellenized Judaism regarded Wisdom (Sophia) as a female principle of mediatorship.

Many of the Gnostic gospels taught that the women who accompanied Jesus were receivers of special revelation hidden from the male disciples and that they functioned as mediators—those who had an "inside track" with God (precursors of later Roman Catholic veneration of Mary and the saints as mediators). It is not surprising, then, that women were attracted to such religions in that they bestowed upon them dignity and self-esteem by accenting and elevating the female principle in deity. And it led women into all sorts of doctrinal and behavioral extremes. Hippolytus of Rome, during the second century A.D., condemned those who "magnify these wretched women [priestesses, prophetesses, goddesses] above the Apostles and every gift of Grace, so that some of them presume to assert that there is in them something superior to Christ."[9]

It was this widespread and deeply held notion of female mediators, both human and divine, that led Paul to affirm categorically that "there is one God, and one mediator also between God and men, the man Christ Jesus" (v. 5, NASB). Furthermore, it is against this general religious background that Paul's specific instructions to women, in the verses that follow, must be read.

After the general entreaty for all people to pray comes more specific applications: "I desire, then, that in every place the men should pray, lifting up holy hands without anger or argument" (v. 8). This is followed by suggesting that "women should dress themselves modestly and decently in suitable clothing . . . as is proper for women who profess reverence for God" (vv. 9-10). Thus Christian women would not be mistaken for the thousands of sacred prostitutes and the devotees of goddess worship, who paraded themselves in gaudy and skimpy attire.

The revolutionary nature of the next verse has been utterly lost to us when Paul says, "Let a woman quietly [or in silence] receive instruction [learn] with entire submissiveness" (v. 11, NASB). We have been conditioned to focus upon "silence" and "submissiveness." Not so the original readers. They heard Paul say something absolutely unprecedented in human history. He not only approves of women receiving instruction, being educated, but also *commands* it. Most translations do not give the verse the imperative force that it has in the Greek. Paul does not say that women "may learn" or "should learn" but that "a woman *must* learn." The Greek verb for learn, *manthano,* is the word used for those attending rabbinical schools.

Suggesting that women possessed the ability to learn, much less had a right to an education, shattered conventional stereotypes. As we have already seen, in Judaism women never had the privilege of even hearing the Law read, much less an opportunity to learn to read and study the Law for themselves. So Paul's unprecedented command enabled women, so long excluded from academic and intellectual pursuits, to pursue an education. They, too, were worthy of both hearing and studying the Word of God, along with the whole range of truth encompassed by it.

Paul's desire that Christian women be instructed in the faith was at once radical in design and difficult in execution. Neither men nor women were ready for it; men were not accustomed to teaching women, and women were not accustomed to the focus and disciplines inherent in learning. And so Paul adds that they should receive instruction "in silence" and "with full submission." Unfortunately, this has a derogatory ring in our culture; we assume it means, "Shut up and listen to what the teacher has to say!" Not so in that day. Paul would have used a different word if he had this in mind, as he did when he told Titus that the troublemakers in his church "must be silenced [epistomizein]" (Titus 1:11).

The word he uses here, however, is *hesuchia*, a beautiful expression in the Greek. In both Jewish and Greek academies, silence was the respectful attention necessary for learning. It was the kind of silence that fell over the crowd, following the uproar precipitated by Paul's visit to the Temple, when he began to speak to them in the Hebrew dialect (Acts 21:40). Simon, son of Gamaliel, Paul's teacher, notes: "All my days have I grown up among the Sages and I have found naught better for a man than silence; and not the expounding [of Law] is the chief thing but the doing [of it]; and he that multiplies words occasions sin."[10]

"Silence" is a quality of spirit, not only repeatedly enjoined by the apostle for men and women, but highly prized by all who desire to learn the deep things of God (1 Thess. 4:11; 2 Thess. 3:12; 1 Tim. 2:2). Ignatius, who was martyred for his faith during the reign of Emperor Trajan, around A.D. 108, wrote that "it is better to be silent and be real, than to talk and to be unreal."[11] Clement of Alexandria, one of the second century's influential Church fathers, saw silence as a virtue for both men and women: "Woman and man are to go to church decently attired, with natural step, embracing silence, possessing unfeigned love, pure in body, pure in heart, fit to pray to God."[12] So the silence enjoined for women is the same as for men. It does not prohibit them from speaking in church or teaching but only applies when they are in the voluntary position of those receiving instruction. Likewise, "with full submission" does not mean "in submission to men" but in submission to the teacher. They should subject themselves quietly to their instructors "as befits women making a claim to godliness" (v. 10, NASB).

We turn now to the verse that has done more to damage the church than any other, the apparent prohibition that has virtually disenfranchised women and has denied them the opportunity to respond fully to the call of God upon their lives and to exercise their special gifts to the fullest: "But I do not allow a woman to teach or exercise authority over a man, but to remain quiet" (v. 12, NASB). It is the biblical fait accompli: the clear, unequivocal basis for denying active ministerial and leadership roles to women. Or is it?

In issuing this particular directive, Paul was speaking to a specific problem that was tearing apart the church at Ephesus. Some form of the word "teaching" (didasko) appears 24 times in 1 and 2 Timothy. Most of its usages occur in the context of "false teaching." It is clear that women were involved in many aspects of the manifold problems that afflicted the church. Young widows were engaging in gossip, living self-indulgent lives, and were turning to occult practices. "Worldly fables" (or "myths") were being spread by "old women" (1 Tim. 4:7, NASB). This occurred because women, denied the disciplined thinking involved in a formal education, were most susceptible to whatever exotic idea or sensational philosophy might catch their attention. They had no background in the Word of God by which to evaluate and judge theological claims or philosophical speculations. So they were being seduced by all sorts of false doctrines and knew no better than to propagate them enthusiastically. Paul recalls, from his own experience, the damage to the gospel of Christ that untutored ignorance can cause (1 Tim. 1:12-14).

For the sake of the integrity of the gospel and the survival of the church, it was necessary for him to lay down verse 12 as an interim limitation. Unable to read or write, having been denied an opportunity to hear and study the Law, they simply did not have the intellectual sophistication or spiritual understanding to be in the position of exercising authority as teachers. Most English translations, however, give the verse a male-chauvinistic force that is unwarranted in the Greek when they render it, as does the King James Version, "But I suffer not a woman to teach, nor to usurp authority over the man, but to be in silence" (v. 12). The verb translated "authority" (authentein) occurs only here in the New Testament. In secular Greek it signified "to commit a murder," "to kill with one's own hands." It suggested monarchial authority where one has life-or-death power over another. It is, therefore, best translated in this context as "dominate." Such dominance is ruled out by Jesus in all Kingdom relationships (Mark 10:42-45). So verse 12 does not forbid women from exercising leadership (exousia) over men but only from domineering them in an aggressive and brazen way.

Paul is not speaking of either men or women as a class here. The verse reads literally, "I do not permit a woman dominance of a man." Since the Greek noun for man (aneir) is in the genitive or possessive case, it should be rendered "of" instead of "over," as it is in most places in the New

Testament. Although commonly translated as a permanent injunction, it does not read that way in the Greek. The Greek verb is in the present active indicative case and ought to be translated, "I am not presently permitting a woman to teach . . ."

Therefore, Paul had no intention whatsoever of laying down a timeless and universal principle prohibiting women from either teaching (preaching) or exercising positions of leadership in the church. Rather, he was cautioning women from assuming roles for which they were neither trained nor equipped at that time. He was encouraging them to be submissive and quiet learners until they had been fully instructed in "true doctrine," after which they would then be qualified and competent to exercise the authority of one who teaches sound doctrine.

Then Paul suggests an analogy whereby they could see what might happen if women persisted in being too aggressive in propagating their ignorance: "For it was Adam who was first created, and then Eve" (v. 13, NASB). Since neither of the Genesis accounts of creation implies a male-dominance hierarchy, we believe that Paul is not suggesting one here either but is merely pointing out a historical fact. "And it was not Adam who was deceived, but the woman being quite deceived, fell into transgression" (v. 14, NASB). Paul is not saying that because Eve was the first one to transgress that somehow her sin was more reprehensible than that of Adam (see Rom. 5:12 ff.).

Rather, Paul is reminding them of the way sin was actually introduced into the world. Eve was the first to fall into transgression, having been "deceived." She then led (taught?) Adam into the very same transgression. Consequently, unlearned women in Ephesus ran the risk of being likewise "deceived" and then of propagating their false doctrines to ignorant and susceptible men, like Adam. Instead of affirming male dominance and devaluing the woman because she was "first deceived," the way Paul put the case, in this passage, casts the man in a negative light as the one who is easily led astray. Even though Adam was first created, he succumbed to the persuasion of a woman's "teaching" without so much as a whisper of objection! Paul is thus paying women a left-handed compliment by acknowledging how effective their teaching can be. His only concern is that they first become dedicated and submissive learners so that later they will be equipped to exercise a responsible role as able teachers of the gospel.[13]

Something else, rather intriguing, may be going on here, giving rise to Paul's reference to Adam and Eve in this context. We learn from the writings of the Church fathers, dating back to the early second century A.D., that they were battling a deeply rooted, widespread, and exceedingly diverse set of heresies that went under the general name of gnosticism (*gnosis* means "knowledge"). These were Christians who, in a sincere but misguided desire to rise to a higher spiritual plane, professed to have inside information that would enable the soul to ascend into the heavenly places and thus escape the corruption of the world represented in all that was physical and material. Blending various elements of Platonic philosophy and Eastern mysticism in with the Christian gospel, they created a vast library of extracanonical gospels and sacred writings that, until recently, could be accessed only through the diatribes against them by the early Christian apologists such as Ignatius, Justin Martyr, Irenaeus, and Tertullian.

An incredible discovery was made in December of 1945, however, which opened up this murky and ancient heresy for closer investigation. Two years before the Dead Sea Scrolls were discovered, copies of more than 50 Gnostic texts dating back to the first centuries of the Christian era were found in the Egyptian desert near the town of Nag Hammadi. They include a collection of early Christian extracanonical gospels and other writings attributed to Jesus, His disciples, and the women who followed Him, such as the Gospel of Thomas, the Gospel of Mary Magdalene, The Secret Book of James, The Secret Book of John, the Apocalypse of Paul, the Dialogue of the Savior, and many more. This was an extraordinary find. Now scholars are able to read the complete Gnostic texts for themselves.[14]

Of particular interest to us is the way some Gnostic sects reinterpreted the Adam and Eve story according to its "deeper meaning." They applied what artists today would call a "creative imagination" to the "shimmering surface of the symbols" in the Genesis account, in an effort to discover its hidden spiritual truth. Rather than being condemned, Eve is praised for her desire to reach for understanding of divine things, represented in the tree of knowledge. Or as Elaine Pagels puts it, "Whereas the orthodox often blamed Eve for the fall and pointed to women's submission as appropriate punishment, gnostics often depicted Eve . . . as the source of spiritual awakening."[15] One such sect had a sacred book called The Gospel of Eve. In another Gnostic text called Reality of the Rulers, Eve rather than Adam is represented as the one who was created first, and thus was the higher and more spiritually enlightened being: "And when he [Adam] saw her [Eve], he said, 'It is you who have given me life: you shall be called Mother of the Living; for it is she who is my Mother. It is she who is the Physician, and the Woman, and She Who Has Given Birth.'"[16]

It is entirely possible that such a rewriting of the Genesis account may have been one of the "myths" being propagated in Ephesus. Desperate to throw off the curse of inferiority and eager for validation as females, some Christian women may have venerated Eve as the higher being, the original spiritual principle and mother of all living. Furthermore, women may have been most responsible for teaching such myths in Ephesus. If this is the case, then Paul's response in 1 Tim. 2:12-13 makes very good sense. We could paraphrase it as follows: "You have been taught by your Gnostic teachers that Eve was formed first and then Adam, and that spiritual enlightenment, which would enable the both of them to become like gods, came through Eve. The Genesis account clearly shows, however, that 'it was Adam who was first created and then Eve.' And it was not Adam who was deceived, but 'the woman being quite deceived, fell into transgression.'"

Then Paul points out that Eve, being deceived, taught Adam "false doctrine." Unfortunately, Adam learned his lesson all too well. He joined Eve in her disobedience, which, in turn, brought sin and death into the world like a flood. Such a chain reaction of being deceived and then teaching false doctrine could likewise destroy the church at Ephesus. It is to break that deadly cycle that Paul says, "But I am not presently allowing a woman to teach false doctrine and exercise domineering authority over men, thus leading them also into sin" (2:12, paraphrase).

Paul's passage on teaching women ends with a curious verse: "Yet she will be saved through childbearing, provided they continue in faith and love and holiness, with modesty" (v. 15). We reject, out of hand, the implication that there is something inherently redemptive about childbearing or that only mothers are worthy of dignity, honor, and respect as equal heirs of the grace of God. Again, a look at the original language helps us sort out this opaque verse. It reads, literally, "But **she** will be saved through **her** childbearing, if **they** remain in faith . . ." The change in pronouns from singular to plural is significant. Who is the **she** who will be saved? Some hold that Paul is referring to Eve, since he has just spoken of her. The salvation being described is not spiritual but physiological; that is, even though Eve died, humanity was preserved (saved) through her childbearing.

A more likely interpretation is that Paul is referring to the protevangelium, the promise made to Eve that one of her "seed" would "bruise you [the serpent] on the head" (Gen. 3:15, NASB). Even as sin came into the world through a woman, so did the Savior come into the world through a woman. This was the interpretation given by Irenaeus in the second century A.D. in *Against Heresies* when he wrote: "And thus also it was that the knot of Eve's disobedience was loosed by the obedience of Mary. For what the virgin Eve had bound fast through unbelief, this did the virgin Mary set free through faith."[17]

Now comes the second pronoun in the verse, "If **they** continue in faith and love and sanctity with self-restraint" (NASB, emphasis added). Who are the **they?** All to whom Paul has been speaking in this extended passage (vv. 8-15), both men and women. The lifting of the curse upon Eve through the obedience of Mary brings salvation and blessing to all, both men and women, as long as **"they** continue in faith and love and sanctity."

In summary, we can confidently affirm that, rather than limiting women's ministerial role in the church, this marvelous passage actually champions it. After all, Paul would hardly have commanded women to be instructed in the faith if he never intended for them to graduate and become teachers and preachers in their own right. His special instructions to women, temporarily restricting them from teaching, had as its ultimate aim that they might indeed become fully informed and spiritually grounded "teachers" of the gospel. To freeze these "interim instructions" as timeless truth, rip them out of their particular historical context, and then make them binding upon all women for all time is to distort the Word of God and pervert the essence of the gospel, which is that "all of you are one in Christ Jesus" (Gal. 3:28).

I feel constrained to point out at least two flagrant flaws in the logic of those who hold that these passages, restricting women's roles in Corinth and Ephesus, represent Paul's permanent and universal intention for the Church. First, it is clear that when it comes to Paul's command, "Let the women keep silent in the churches" (1 Cor. 14:34), **nobody takes it literally!** To the contrary, even the most patriarchal traditionalist churches would be irreparably crippled if women ceased to "speak"—that is, witness, testify, sing, teach, counsel, comfort, encourage, and serve in all sorts of ministries.

Now here is the question: If we are not willing to interpret this injunction against women speaking in church literally, then on what basis do we draw the line at the point of women preaching? If women cannot be trusted to preach and teach the Word to adults, should they be allowed to shoulder the bulk of responsibility for leading and teaching children who are at the most impressionable and vulnerable stage of their lives?

Second, most Evangelicals who hold that 1 Tim. 2:11-15 represents a permanent injunction against women in ministerial leadership roles stop short of making the same claim for the verses immediately preceding (vv. 9-10), which specifically forbid women from braiding their hair and from wearing gold, pearls, or costly garments. Likewise, Paul's counsel to Timothy, in this same letter, to "no longer drink water exclusively, but use a little wine for the sake of your stomach and your frequent ailments" (5:23, NASB) is not taken as a command for all ministers to partake of alcoholic beverages. It is understood that this represented sound medicinal advice appropriate to that time and situation where water was not fit to drink. The same could be said for Paul's directives concerning slaves and masters (6:1-2) and his long instructions on how to deal with widows (5:9-16).

On what hermeneutical grounds, therefore, are most of Paul's specific instructions to that particular church at Ephesus deemed as applicable only to that time, culture, and specific local situation, and yet 1 Tim. 2:12 is lifted up as a law binding upon all churches for all time? Once we have placed these texts in context and have candidly faced up to what was going on in the troubled churches to which they were addressed, we can no longer, in good conscience, rip them out of context and use them as scriptural cudgels to hammer women into a position of subservient passivity and inferior standing within the Body of Christ.

We began our study by noting that positions supporting male dominance and female subordination in the home and church are indeed "biblical"; that is, they can be supported by isolated texts in the Bible. Our question from the beginning of this study, however, has been this: Do these texts, which have been used to institutionalize discrimination against women, represent the overall revelation of Scripture, **which finds its fullest and final expression in Jesus?**

Our analysis thus far leads us to only one possible answer: **No!** These texts do not represent God's original intention for the race. Neither are they representative of the overall teaching and practice of the apostle Paul. Most decisively, they find no support whatsoever in the teaching or example of Jesus. And, for the Christian interpreter, **the life, teachings, and example of Jesus are the ultimate criteria by which everything else in the Bible is evaluated and judged.**

It is important, finally, to see that our analysis of these problem passages does not represent an off-the-wall, strange hermeneutic but is in line with some of the best evangelical scholarship today. The "Danvers Statement" cited earlier, which reaffirms patriarchal hierarchy in church and home, sent a shock wave rippling through the evangelical community when it was first published in early 1989.[18] While praised by traditionalists, it alarmed many other leading Evangelicals who saw it as a giant leap backward into a narrow and truncated distortion of biblical teaching concerning women. Furthermore, they perceived it to be a reactionary effort justifying the continuing scandal of discrimination against women in church and society.

Consequently, these concerned Evangelicals banded together and formed a new organization called Christians for Biblical Equality. Supporting it is an impressive and growing coalition of scholars and leaders that also reads like a who's who list of Evangelicals, including Myron Augsburger, F. F. Bruce, Donald Buteyn, Anthony Campolo, Edward Dayton, Paul De Vries, Gary W. Demarest, Louis Evans, Vernon Grounds, David Allen Hubbard, Richard C. Halverson, David L. McKenna, Donn D. Moomaw, Ronald J. Sider, Lewis Smedes, Mary Stewart Van Leeuwen, Timothy Weber, and Kenneth Kantzer, senior editor of *Christianity Today*.[19] They, too, have published a statement that upholds the position we have advanced and defended regarding full biblical equality, in home, church, and society for women and men. We conclude our analysis of the texts that seem to restrict the role of women in church with their affirmation regarding "community":

> 1. In the church, spiritual gifts of women and men are to be recognized, developed and used in serving and teaching ministries at all levels of involvement: as small group leaders, counselors, facilitators, administrators, ushers, communion servers, and board members, and in pastoral care, teaching, preaching, and worship.
>
> In so doing, the church will honor God as the source of spiritual gifts. The church will also fulfill

God's mandate of stewardship without the appalling loss to God's kingdom that results when half of the church's members are excluded from positions of responsibility.

2. In the church, public recognition is to be given to both women and men who exercise ministries of service and leadership. In so doing, the church will model the unity and harmony that should characterize the community of believers. In a world fractured by discrimination and segregation, the church will dissociate itself from worldly or pagan devices designed to make women feel inferior for being female. It will help prevent their departure from the church or their rejection of the Christian faith.[20]

7.

Evangelical Roots of Biblical Feminism

*I*t comes as a surprise to most Evangelicals—if not a shock—to discover that the feminist movement that has completely revolutionized male-female relationships in the 20th century has its origins—not in Marxist socialism, nor in secular humanism, nor even in theological liberalism, but in the great evangelical and holiness revivals of the last two centuries. Donald Dayton asserts, in *Discovering an Evangelical Heritage,* that "modern revivalism gave birth to the women's rights movement."[1] He points out that "a recent anthology of *The Feminist Papers* collected by Alice Rossi begins to set the record straight by tracing the roots of American feminism to the revivalism of Charles G. Finney and the reform movements it spawned."[2] Janette Hassey, in her study of "Evangelical Women in Public Ministry Around the Turn of the Century" agrees: "Evangelical feminism in America first surfaced in the mid-nineteenth century and accelerated at the turn of the century. . . . [It] mobilized women and freed leaders such as Phoebe Palmer and Frances Willard to preach."[3]

These movements, however, were foreshadowed in the rise of the Quakers, but even more so in the great evangelical revival that swept across England under John Wesley's leadership and leapt the Atlantic to become a major catalyst in the Great Awakenings. These in turn unleashed an avalanche of social reform movements, including the drive for temperance, the abolition of slavery, and the right of women to vote. There was an implicit leveling force in vital, experiential Christianity that paralleled the egalitarian philosophies and democratizing revolutions that were challenging monarchies and destroying autocracies all across Europe.

Even more important, however, was the dramatic shift from confessional to experiential religion. Ecclesiastical hierarchies, which vested religious authority in trained clergy and closed sacramental systems, gave way to a more immediate spiritual authority in which all believers might freely participate, validated by the "inner light" and the "witness of the Spirit." First George Fox in the 1600s, and then the Wesley brothers in the 1700s, encouraged and empowered the laity to assume a more active role in the life of the church. One did not need official ecclesiastical ordination to engage in preaching, evangelism, and the care of souls. The call of God evidenced by positive spiritual results was the final validation of fitness for ministry. With the increasing dissolution of the walls between clergy and laity came also the removal of the historic barriers locking women out of full participation in the life and ministry of the church. Since such a high premium was placed upon spiritual sensitivity, it was inevitable that new roles would open for women, since it became abundantly apparent that the Holy Spirit was no respecter of gender when it came to spiritual things. Let us trace this historical development.

THE QUAKERS

As a result of a profound religious experience, George Fox (1624-91) began to preach that God's revelation is received not only from the Scriptures—though they are a true Word of God—but also from an "inner light" that en-

lightens every true disciple. Fox's preaching attracted a nu-
cleus of followers who would become the Society of
Friends or Quakers. Fox initiated a democratic form of
worship marked by simplicity and spontaneity, in which
every believer could speak, pray, or sing as the Spirit
moved. He rejected a professional clergy, deferential titles,
and all distinctions that would elevate certain classes of
people over others.[4] Men and women, rich and poor,
learned and unlearned were equally the "people of God."
All were encouraged to participate fully in the life and
ministry of the church as led by the Spirit. In their wedding ceremonies, Quakers rejected traditional vows where
the wife promised to "love, honor, and obey" her husband
and replaced it with expressions of mutual submission and
partnership.[5] In his position of leadership, Fox set the example by submitting himself to the counsel and advice of
women. It is not surprising, therefore, that women were
drawn to this new religious movement from the beginning.

Most radical of Fox's innovations was his willingness
to open the preaching ministry to women as well as to
men. By eliminating a professional ministerial class, the
way was opened for every believer to participate in worship ministry and leadership. By disposing of the sacraments as part of worship, there was no need for an ordained clergy to administer them. While Fox never
ordained anyone, he and his movement did "acknowledge" certain members, both male and female, upon
whom the Spirit of God came with unusual power and in
whom exceptional gifts for preaching and pastoral care
were evident. He made a strong defense of women preachers in this 1656 treatise: "If *Christ* be in the Female as well
as in the Male, is not he the same? And may not the Spirit
of *Christ* speak in the Female as well as in the Male? Is he
there to be limited? Who is it that dare limit the Holy one

of Israel? For the Light is the same in the Male, and in the Female, which cometh from *Christ.*"[6]

One of his early converts, Elizabeth Hooten, became the Quaker's first woman preacher. She did not shrink from challenging an Anglican priest on doctrinal matters, and she refused to kneel before King Charles II. For such behavior she was beaten and imprisoned several times. She preached throughout the American colonies. While visiting a fellow Quaker in Boston, she was publicly whipped and banned from ever entering the city again. She later served as a missionary to the West Indies.

Fox's most eminent early convert was Margaret Fell. Her home became a prominent meeting place for Quaker preachers. She wrote on behalf of the movement, served as its financial secretary, became an important adviser to Fox and, in later years, became his wife following the death of her first husband. While in prison she wrote a pamphlet defending women's right to preach, which declared its central thesis in its extended title: "Women's Speaking Justified, Proved and Allowed of by the Scriptures, and such as speak by the Spirit and Power of the Lord Jesus, and how Women were the first that preached the Tidings of the Resurrection of Jesus and were sent by Christ's Own Command, before He ascended to the Father, John 20:17."[7] In it she makes three compelling points: (1) Men and women were equal in status before the Fall in Genesis and were restored to that equality by Jesus. (2) Paul's instructions prohibiting women from speaking were directed to specific problem churches that had not yet received the fullness of God's grace. (3) God himself anointed many women, including Mary the mother of Jesus, to be witnesses and proclaimers of the Word.[8]

Even though Fell's line of interpretation was regarded as heretical, Quakers defended it on the basis of the "inner light" that enabled them to understand the Scriptures, not only in their literal sense but in their spiritual sense as well. The Quakers' most illustrious convert, William Penn (1644-1718), led some 800 Quakers to the American Colonies, eventually obtaining the grant of Pennsylvania in 1681, which allowed him to begin his unique colonial "Holy Experiment." Quaker women, who played a prominent role in spreading the Quaker version of the gospel, were the only female preachers during the colonial era. Some even returned to England and Ireland as missionaries.

English Quakers, branded as Dissenters, paid a fearful price to hold their "heretical" doctrines and exercise their unorthodox form of worship. Over 400 died in prison, and many more were ruined financially. Even in the colonies, women were subjected to persecution. Mary Tompkins and Alice Ambrose were put in public stocks, whipped, and expelled from Virginia. Mary Dyer, another Quaker preacher, was hanged in Boston, in 1660, after refusing a reprieve conditioned upon her promise to leave and never enter the city again.[9]

Though the main body of Friends tended toward quietism as the church matured, an activist wing emerged in the late 1800s in the West, which identified with holiness causes such as programmed ministries, missions, education, and women's right to preach. Southern California Quakers organized the Training School for Christian Workers in 1899, which later became Whittier College. Its first president was a prominent woman preacher, Mary A. Hill.

The Quakers were the first since apostolic times to make such a large place for women in their church and have the longest unbroken history of women preachers of any denomination. Their example and influence contributed mightily to the equal rights movement that finally resulted in the historic adoption of the Nineteenth Amendment in 1920, giving women the right to vote.

JOHN WESLEY

John Wesley (1703-91), a devotedly conventional Anglican priest and Oxford don, experienced a slow but complete about-face in regard to women preachers. This "conversion" did not come easily for him, given the bias against women that he inherited and that was the unquestioned orthodoxy of his day. As late as 1748, ten years after his own heartwarming experience, he argued strongly against the Quaker practice of allowing women to preach by citing the two classic Pauline texts prohibiting women from speaking and teaching.[10] What compelled him to gradually change his mind were at least three factors.

First, his mother, Susanna Wesley, coming from a long line of religious nonconformists, had an enormous impact upon him. In addition to her godly life and maternal influence, she broke new ground for women. So consumed was she by a desire to see the salvation of souls that she ventured forth into forbidden regions. She turned her family worship into a Sunday evening service to which she invited friends and neighbors. She became its worship leader, Bible teacher, and exhorter. Her gifts were so evident and her ministry so Spirit-anointed that the handful who initially responded grew into a congregation of over 200. Her husband, Samuel, a proper Anglican minister, questioned the propriety of her activities but could not deny the blessing of God upon her labors. He not only gave his approval but went to her defense when the local Anglican rector objected. Once the great evangelical revival began to sweep across England, Susanna encouraged John and Charles to permit both lay men and women to hold leadership responsibilities and preach. It was her example as a woman preacher, though never ordained, that contributed significantly to ultimately breaking down John's reservations.

Second, though ever loyal to Anglican doctrine and traditions, Wesley was a pragmatist. He recognized that revival movements cut their own channels and called for fresh methods. In addition to such new and strange practices as "field preaching" and setting hymns to popular tunes, he gave the church back to the laity through the aegis of the small-group class meeting. Wesley encouraged both men and women to sing, pray, testify, exhort, remonstrate, and encourage one another in the Society meetings. This represented a radical departure from convention in that women ordinarily did not actively participate in religious services. Such freedom proved to be so compelling that women far outnumbered men in early Methodist Societies.

Third, it became evident that God was mightily using women in evangelism, exhortation, and even preaching, whether or not he gave them his blessing. As early as 1739, the year following his own heartwarming experience, Wesley appointed women as class leaders in Bristol and allowed them to exhort so long as they did not take a text and discourse upon it. The line between exhortation and preaching, however, became exceedingly blurred as can be seen in this letter from Mrs. Sarah Crosby to Mr. Wesley:

> In the evening I expected to meet about thirty persons in class; but to my great surprise there came near two hundred. I found an awful, loving sense of the Lord's presence, and much love to the people. . . . I was not sure whether it was right for me to exhort in so public a manner, and yet I saw it impracticable to meet all these people by way of speaking particularly to each individual. I, therefore, gave out a hymn, and prayed, and told them part of what the Lord had done for myself, persuading them to flee from all sin.[11]

Sarah realized that she had come perilously close to preaching and was troubled by engaging in an activity prohibited by the Methodists at that time. Wesley responded that "I do not see that you have broken any law,"[12] but he suggested that she confine herself to prayers, testimonies, and short exhortations. Her continuing success, however, caused him to change his mind, and he gave her his permission to preach after recognizing her "extraordinary call." She became Methodism's first duly recognized woman preacher. When Wesley saw that the Holy Spirit increasingly honored the preaching of women with converts, and blessed their labors with abundant spiritual fruit, he could no longer withhold his general approval.[13]

While it is difficult to determine precisely when he made the final move from qualified approval to positive encouragement for women to preach, Wesley scholar Paul Chilcote believes that it occurred sometime after receiving an extraordinary letter in 1771 from one of his most productive class leaders, Mary Bosanquet. In it she makes a lengthy defense of women's right to preach. Her reasoned argument is based upon Scripture. Undoubtedly aware of how Mr. Wesley had not been able to get around the so-called prohibitive passages in 1 Corinthians 14 and 1 Timothy 2, she begins there by stating that these are directed only to certain women who were causing trouble in two specific problem churches and were not intended to be applied to all women generally. Otherwise these texts would be in direct contradiction to 1 Cor. 11:5 where Paul acknowledges women "praying and prophesying" (NASB) with no word of condemnation, as well as other passages where he commends women and speaks of them as his "fellow workers in Christ Jesus" (Rom. 16:3, NASB; see also Rom. 16:1-9; Phil. 4:2-3; Col. 4:15). By pointing to the examples of the handmaiden of 2 Samuel 20, Deborah, the Samaritan woman at the well, Mary the mother of Jesus, and the women who first proclaimed the Resurrection, she also rejects the notion that preaching is inconsistent with the modesty required of women professing godliness.

In the decade prior to Wesley's death in 1791, there was a great flowering of women preachers within Methodism all over England. Mary Fletcher often preached to crowds of 2,000 to 3,000. Upon the death of her husband, Wesley encouraged her to preach as much as possible. He described her preaching as "fire, conveying both light and heat to all that heard her. . . . Her manner of speaking [is] smooth, easy, and natural, even when the sense is deep and strong."[14] It is interesting to note that in deference to those who objected to "female preachers," she preached from the pulpit steps and not the pulpit itself. Chilcote summarizes this final stage of development as follows:

> As a result of Wesley's changing attitude about the role of female preachers in his movement and the testimony of many witnesses to the abundant fruit of their labor, the English Methodist Conference was eventually led to recognize officially a number of these exceptional women. In these later years, when Wesley was asked why he encouraged certain of his female devotees in this practice, the elderly sage replied simply, "Because God owns them in the conversion of sinners, and who am I that I should withstand God."[15]

In his study of early Methodist women, Earl Kent Brown states that "we have varying amounts of information on 110 women whose active Methodist lives overlapped Mr. Wesley's."[16] By "active" he means women who distinguished themselves as preachers, class leaders, advisers, and counselors. Adam Clarke, Bible scholar and a close Wesley associate, said this about women preachers: "Under the blessed spirit of Christianity, they have equal **rights,** equal **privileges,** and equal **blessing,** and let me add, they are equally **useful.**"[17] Methodist historian Robert F. Wearmouth points out that before Wesley it was unheard of in England for women to hold positions of leadership in government or church. Wearmouth goes on to say, "It might be claimed that *the emancipation of womanhood began with him.*"[18]

Sadly, it nearly ended with him as well, for upon Wesley's death in 1791, bitter controversy exploded among his followers over the issue of women preaching. Within a decade of his death, women were either formally forbidden to preach or were so restricted that it became almost impossible to function as before. Nevertheless, a door had been opened that could not be closed permanently. Methodists today lead all denominations in both numbers and percentages of women ministers. Likewise, the seeds of equality for women had been planted that would germinate and sprout in historic new ways in the next century, particularly in America.

CHARLES FINNEY

Charles Finney (1792-1875) has been called the father of American revivalism. Like Wesley, Finney was an innovator. He was the first to popularize the "protracted meeting" and the first to employ the use of "the anxious bench" for those under conviction of sin, later known as "the altar call." Most revolutionary—and controversial—of his "new measures" was his practice of encouraging women to pray, testify, and speak in mixed assemblies. This eventually opened the door wide for women lecturers and preachers. Along with abolitionist Theodore Weld, Finney encouraged women to take the platform in speaking out against slavery. From this time forward, the abolition and feminist movements proceeded hand in hand. Since Gal. 3:28 declared that "there is no longer . . . slave or free, there is no longer male and female; for all of you are one in Christ Jesus," then why not press for the enfranchisement of women as well as freedom for the slaves?

Finney influenced evangelist Dwight L. Moody who worked with and encouraged a number of women preachers including Frances Willard (1839-98), a powerful speaker. Since church pulpits were closed to women, she devoted herself to the cause of temperance, serving as a founder and first president of the Women's Christian Temperance Union. She used this platform to promote the cause of equal rights and women's suffrage. She published a strong defense of female ministry titled *Women in the Pulpit*. In a letter to Mrs. D. L. Moody, Willard expressed her deeply held conviction succinctly:

> All my life I have been devoted to the advancement of women in education and opportunity. I firmly believe God has a work for them to do as evangelists, as bearers of Christ's message to the ungospeled, to the prayer-meeting, to the church generally and the world at large. . . . It is therefore my dearest wish to help break down the barriers of prejudice that keep them silent. . . . As in the day of Pentecost, so now, let men and women in perfectly impartial fashion participate in all services conducted in His name in whom "there is neither bond nor free, male nor female, but all are one."[19]

OBERLIN COLLEGE

Oberlin College in Ohio has the distinction of being **the first coeducational college in the history of humankind.** Oberlin was founded in the early 1830s to perpetuate both revivalism and the social reforms of Charles G. Finney. Finney served as professor of theology before succeeding Asa Mahan in the presidency. Oberlin was at the forefront of three historic social movements of the mid-19th century: the peace movement, the abolition of slavery, and the women's rights crusade. Donald Dayton argues that "feminist exegesis" grew out of abolitionism. He notes that

> those who mastered Theodore Weld's "Bible argument against slavery" and learned to defend the egalitarian

and liberationist "spirit" of the Bible against status quo literal interpretations, found that the same arguments could be used in support of the women's movement. Even Galatians 3:28 seemed to conjoin the issues by declaring that "There is neither . . . bond nor free, there is neither male nor female; for ye are all one in Christ Jesus."[20]

Oberlin graduated many women who became leaders in both the abolitionist and feminist movements of the 19th century, including Antoinette Brown, the first woman to be ordained and installed as a pastor in a mainline Protestant church in America, or anywhere else. Another was her classmate and eventual sister-in-law, Lucy Stone, a pioneer woman suffragist, abolitionist, and founder of the National Woman's Rights Convention. When Lucy married Henry Blackwell, she broke social convention by retaining her maiden name and became known as "Mrs. Stone." She and her husband signed a statement that guaranteed that she would be regarded as "an independent, rational being." In 1870, she and her husband founded the *Woman's Journal*, the principal suffragist paper.

Antoinette's and Lucy's sisters-in-law were Elizabeth Blackwell, the first woman doctor in the history of medicine, and Emily Blackwell, who founded the New York Infirmary for Women and Children, America's first hospital for women.[21] Asa Mahan, Oberlin's first president, was so proud of this record that he suggested an epitaph for his tombstone: "The first man, in the history of the race who conducted women, in connection with members of the opposite sex, through a full course of liberal education, and conferred upon them the high degrees which had hitherto been the exclusive prerogatives of men."[22]

ANTOINETTE BROWN

As America's first regularly ordained woman minister, Antoinette L. Brown (1825-1921) deserves special attention. After graduating from Oberlin in 1847, she returned a year later to take its three-year course in theology. This created a crisis among the faculty since no women had ever studied theology at Oberlin before. Furthermore, there was no precedent of any college, university, or seminary admitting a woman to a preministerial course. Even her family opposed her; her father and brother ceased to support her financially. Though she and her friend, Lettice Smith, were grudgingly allowed to attend classes, they were not given degrees, nor were they permitted to participate in commencement exercises. Their names did not appear in the alumni catalogue as graduates of the theological class of 1850. It was decades before Oberlin rectified this omission and included them.

Denied access to pulpits, Antoinette lectured with great success, drawing large crowds. One of her ardent supporters, Horace Greeley, founder of *The New York Tribune*, offered her a pulpit in New York City with a large salary. She declined, considering herself too inexperienced for a metropolitan church, and instead accepted the call to a struggling little Congregational church at South Butler, N.Y. It was there that she was ordained by Wesleyan Methodist leader Luther Lee in 1853.

She resigned as pastor shortly before her marriage to Samuel Blackwell in 1855, believing such a position to be incompatible with her responsibilities as wife and, eventually, mother of six daughters. Nevertheless she remained active as a much-sought-after lecturer and preacher. She also wrote 10 books. At 75 years of age she accepted the call as pastor of the Unitarian church in Elizabeth, N.J., where she served with distinction until she was 90. Oberlin awarded her the honorary degree of doctor of divinity when she was 83, the first such degree ever bestowed upon a woman by any institution of higher learning. By the time of her death at 96, there were more than 3,000 licensed and ordained women ministers in the United States.[23]

PHOEBE PALMER

The cause of women's rights received a mighty thrust from the work of Phoebe Palmer, a physician's wife and a Methodist lay evangelist. She is often referred to as the "Mother of the Holiness Movement." For 20 years she conducted the Tuesday Meeting for the Promotion of Holiness in her home. Hundreds of Methodist preachers were sanctified under her influence, including five bishops. Her success inspired scores of other women to initiate holiness meetings in their homes as well. It opened up an opportune door of ministry to women for spiritual leadership. She played a major role in the revival of 1857-58, preached to great crowds all over the country, and with her husband, Walter, engaged in 4 years of fruitful evangelistic campaigns all across the British Isles.[24]

Mrs. Palmer published a 421-page book defending the right of women to preach, *The Promise of the Father*. She based her argument primarily upon the prophecy of Joel, quoted by Peter in his Pentecost sermon, which declared that in the age of the Spirit both men and women would prophesy. This became the principal scriptural justification for women preachers throughout the 19th and early 20th centuries. She makes an eloquent plea that women should be allowed to become full participants in the ministry of the church in view of the fact that more and more of them were preaching under the direct influence of the Holy Spirit. She appealed to John Wesley who licensed women to preach, and blamed "the iron hand of Calvinism" for choking the work of the Spirit by artificially limiting women's work on the basis of gender. She chides men, particularly clergy, for keeping women down, and she invites women to claim their power and rights in Christ, as is evident in this sample:

> The Lord our God is one Lord. The same in-dwelling spirit of might which fell upon Mary and the other women on the glorious day that ushered in the present dispensation still falls upon God's daughters. Not a few of the daughters of the Lord Almighty have, in obedience to the command of the Saviour, tarried at Jerusalem; and, the endowment from on high having fallen upon them, the same impelling power which constrained Mary and the other women to speak as the Spirit gave utterance impels them to testify of Christ. . . . And how do these divinely-baptized disciples stand ready to obey these impelling influences? Answer, ye thousands of Heaven-touched lips, whose testimonies have so long been repressed in the assemblies of the pious! Yes, answer, ye thousands of female disciples, of every Christian land, whose pent-up voices have so long, under the pressure of these man-made restraints, been uttered in groanings before God.[25]

Mrs. Palmer was also active in establishing inner-city missions, relief work, and a settlement house for the poor in New York City. She served as editor for *Guide to Holiness* and engaged in extensive writing. She is credited with bringing in excess of 25,000 people to Christ for salvation. She also encouraged many women to assert themselves in preaching. Included among these were Frances Willard and Catherine Booth.

THE SALVATION ARMY

Catherine Mumford Booth who, with her husband, William, cofounded the Salvation Army, was a powerful and popular preacher. In Portsmouth, England, crowds averaging over 1,000 came nightly for 17 weeks to hear her preach. Often she spoke to much larger gatherings. When her daughters were grown and married, they kept their family name and were among the first to use a hyphenated married name: Booth-Tucker, Booth-Clibborn, and so on. From its beginning, the Army welcomed, trained, and commissioned women as officers (ministers). In 1934 Evangeline Booth was elected as general of the Salvation Army, the first woman to lead any major denomination in Protestant history.

THE BIBLE COLLEGE MOVEMENT

Historian Janette Hassey asserts that "Bible institutes played an important part in shaping turn-of-the-century Evangelicalism . . . [and] provided a major training ground for Evangelical women of that era who entered public ministry."[26] Albert B. Simpson, founder of the Christian and Missionary Alliance church, established North America's first Bible institute in 1883 in New York City, later relocated to Nyack. He gave women a prominent place in church ministry and leadership. He included women on his institute's executive board, employed them as Bible professors, and was proud of his school's record of sending forth women as missionaries, evangelists, and pastors. The May 1888 graduation prize for excellence in preaching went to a woman.[27] Unfortunately, the General Council of the C&MA reversed its historic position in 1981, and no longer allows women to be ordained. Furthermore, all women's ministries must now be conducted under the authority of a male elder.

Among the many Bible colleges Hassey surveys, the formation of Moody Bible Institute is instructive. It would never had been established had it not been for Emma Dryer, a Bible teacher and friend of D. L. Moody, who strongly and insistently encouraged him to do so. Since his extensive evangelistic campaigns kept him away from Chicago, he appointed her to supervise the Chicago Bible Work in his church. Most of her earliest efforts concentrated on women whom she trained as Bible readers. They served as city missionaries, evangelized the poor, distributed tracts, visited the sick, organized home prayer meetings, and established morning schools for children. From this evolved the Bible Institute of the Chicago Evangelization Society in 1889, renamed Moody Bible Institute in 1900. Moody continuously pled for both men and women to respond to God's call to preach and minister, especially to the poor.

An extension department was organized in 1887 to promote Bible conferences, supply evangelists for revival meetings, and provide churches with guest preachers. Women were not only accepted as preachers and Bible teachers but also sought out by churches. By 1928 over 250,000 people had attended 25 Moody Bible Institute-sponsored conferences around the country. For 40 years Moody graduated women who "openly served as pastors, evangelists, pulpit supply preachers, Bible teachers, and even in the ordained ministry."[28]

Unfortunately, the sexist-chauvinist "spirit of this present Fundamentalist age" claimed another great evangelical institution, as is clear in this statement published by the administration of the Moody Bible Institute in 1979: "Our policy has been and is that we do not endorse or encourage the ordination of women nor do we admit women to our Pastoral Training Major."[29]

THE HOLINESS DENOMINATIONS

It was the denominations produced by the mid-19th-century holiness revivals that most consistently raised feminism to a central principle of church life. The Wesleyan Methodists began to ordain women in the 1860s, nearly a century in advance of the mainline Methodist church. Donald Dayton shows that there is a "striking connection" between the Wesleyan Methodists and the women's rights movement: "The Seneca Falls meeting of 1848 that launched the movement and first called for the franchise for women was held in a Wesleyan Methodist church—apparently because only the abolitionist denomination was at all receptive to such radical ideas. (Even here there was some equivocation. When the women arrived for the meeting, they found the building locked and had to climb in through a window!)"[30]

When the Church of God, Anderson, Ind., was established in the 1880s, 25 percent of its ministers and delegates were women. In a letter to a "sister in Christ," early Church of God leader F. G. Smith spelled out the movement's rationale for not only permitting but encouraging women to preach:

> Again, I call your attention to the organization of the church by the Holy Spirit. A man is an evangelist because he has the gift of evangelizing. It is not because he is a man, but because he has that particular gift. The gift itself is the proof of his calling. If a woman has divine gifts fitting her for a particular work in the church, that is the proof, and the only proof needed, that is her place. Any other basis of qualification than divine gifts is superficial and arbitrary and ignores the divine plan of organization and government in the church.[31]

The Pilgrim Holiness church, founded by Seth Rees (father of Paul S. Rees, prominent in the founding of the National Association of Evangelicals in the 1940s), opened wide the door to women preachers who comprised 30 percent of its ordained elders in its early decades. Rees's wife served with him as copastor and coevangelist. Against those who opposed women preachers, Rees countered, "Nothing but jealousy, prejudice, bigotry, and a stingy love for bossing in men have prevented woman's public recognition by the Church."[32]

THE CHURCH OF THE NAZARENE

From the time Phineas Bresee organized the first Church of the Nazarene in Los Angeles in 1895, women preachers and leaders played a vital role in the life of the young denomination. The first printed flier produced by the new church advertising services listed six deaconesses, including Mrs. W. S. Knott who became the first woman ordained by Bresee. She and her husband founded the Mateo Street Mission, which later became the Compton Avenue Church. Bresee organized a Spokane mission founded by Elsie Wallace as First Church of the Nazarene in 1905, ordained her and appointed her as pastor. She went on to organize Nazarene churches in Ashland, Oreg.; Boise, Idaho; Walla Walla and Seattle, Wash., serving as pastor for brief periods of time in most of these. She holds the distinction of being the only woman to have served as a district superintendent in North America, having been appointed by Bresee to serve out a term vacated when C. Warren Jones went to Japan as a missionary.

Typical of the holiness groups that formed the Church of the Nazarene union at Pilot Point, Tex., in 1908, was the New Testament Church of Christ. It was organized by evangelist Robert Lee Harris in 1893 after he withdrew from the Methodist church. While slowly succumbing to tuberculosis, he encouraged several women, including his wife, to preach when he was ill. When he passed away in 1894, the fledgling church began to spread throughout the South on the wings of these women preachers "whose ordination knew no apostolic succession."[33] One of these, Mrs. Fannie McDowell Hunter, published *Women Preachers* (1905) in which a dozen of her coworkers presented their defense of women preachers in autobiographical form.[34] At the time of the 1908 union, all of the preachers of the New Testament Church of Christ were women.

Three of the four regional groups comprising the 1908 Pilot Point union ordained women to the preaching ministry. The one exception was J. O. McClurkan who, even though 39 percent of his Pentecostal Mission's evangelists were women, objected to their ordination on "scriptural grounds." Six years after his death, his widow was ordained.[35]

At the time when the four main groups of holiness churches united, approximately 15 percent of the licensed and ordained elders were women. This swelled to over 20 percent during the next four decades, with some regions reporting more than 30 percent of their ministers as women. Yet the Church of the Nazarene's acceptance of women in the pulpit was not without its vocal critics, prompting this spirited 1930 *Herald of Holiness* editorial in which General Superintendent J. B. Chapman defends the young denomination's stance: "The fact is that God calls men and women to preach the gospel, and when He does so call them, they should gladly obey Him and members of the church and of the ministry should encourage and help them in the fulfillment of their task. This is the teaching of the New Testament, the logic of the new dispensation, the position of the Church of the Nazarene."[36]

In her definitive study of early women preachers in the Church of the Nazarene, Rebecca Laird identifies the common threads that characterized their lives and ministries. First, there was a deep conviction that they had been called of God and empowered to preach by the sanctifying grace of the indwelling Holy Spirit. Second, each struggled with the call, knowing that it was often deemed inappropriate and out of step with family, church, and societal expectations. Third, they evidenced a willingness to go ahead and preach, wherever and whenever they could, not waiting for official sanction. In every instance, licensing and ordination was granted after the fact of their demonstrated gifts and fruitfulness in preaching. Fourth, most planted the churches they served through their own evangelistic efforts. Rarely was a woman called to pastor an established church or lead an existing institution. Fifth, they formed informal support networks among themselves. This was essential to their long-term survival in ministry, given the fact that even in the best of times, they battled against traditional patriarchal attitudes at all levels.[37]

Sadly, it has been a losing battle. Women comprise about 10 percent of currently licensed and ordained ministers, with less than 1 percent serving as pastors. Most hold no full-time position in the church. Noting the gradual demise of this noble heritage of equality and liberty for women, General Superintendent William M. Greathouse sounded an alarm when he wrote: "The partial eclipse of women ministers in the church of today is lamentable. It reflects the influx of teachings and theologies which are in basic disagreement with our historic biblical position." He goes on to affirm, however, that **the gospel is the Magna Charta for women's ministry.** Once again the Lord is pouring out His Spirit on His handmaidens in the Church of the Nazarene and calling them to preach."[38]

The question is: Are we ready to receive them?

· 8

Setting Women Free
for Ministry

*I*t is ironic that evangelicalism, which gave birth to the women's rights movement, not only has deserted its offspring but has become its most vitriolic opponent. Why such a reversal? The reasons are many and complex. We have already dealt extensively with the first: namely, the rise of biblical literalism in which isolated verses have been ripped out of context and used as clubs to bludgeon women back into their traditional status of subservience, submissiveness, and silence.

A second reason for Evangelicals distancing themselves from feminism is theological. It is rooted in a concept of God weighted heavily, if not totally, on the side of male metaphors. From this arises a renewed commitment to the idea that men can better represent God before the congregation than can women.

Third, and even more critical, is the misunderstanding of, and virulent reaction to, the feminist movement. Feminism, like most movements, is defined by its extremists on the one hand and its critics on the other. And women preachers are often lumped together with them. Feminism has been blamed for all that is wrong in marriages, families, and society today. Women engaged in professional ministry only accentuate the problem, in the eyes of these critics.

The final reason for the eclipse of women in ministry is practical: that is, doors of opportunity have increasingly closed to them—sometimes noisily, sometimes quietly, but nonetheless tightly. Jesus' warning that "many are called, but few are chosen" (Matt. 22:14) is certainly the case in that many gifted Christian women continue to be called by God but few are allowed to enter into ministry by our male-dominated and -controlled church. Our entrenched resistance to them has not yielded to a quiet, reasonable approach. Rather, we force them to consider the aggressive, divisive, and militant strategies of some secular feminists. We leave them with no other choices except stridency or departure.

Two thousand years of Church history have shown that heroic women have, in every generation, made sustained, noble, and vital contributions to the Church and the cause of Christ.[1] Yet, like caged eagles, women have been restricted from stretching their wings to the fullest. They have been unable to soar into the stratosphere of the "upward call of God in Christ Jesus" (Phil. 3:14, NASB). Sadly, the Body of Christ has been deprived of the full measure of what they, and only they, can offer.

Rena Yocom, a diaconal minister in the United Methodist church, tells the story about two elderly sisters who, one Christmas, received a silk flower arrangement from an estranged sister. They examined the gift and decided they did not want it. The arrangement did not match anything in their house. Besides, they judged that such an expensive gift was inappropriate given their sister's small pension. And so they "ungifted" the gift, sending it back to their sister. Then she draws the analogy: "Women have time and time again had the painful experience of the church 'ungifting' our gifts. Our gifts are often deemed undesirable because they do not match the ecclesial furniture or because they are not like anything anybody has envisioned. . . . This 'ungifting' is denial, denial of the giver as well as the gifts."[2]

The time has come to "proclaim release to the captives" (Luke 4:18), strike the chains, and throw open the gates that the "King of glory may come in" (Ps. 24:7) on the wings of words uttered in the feminine voice. We cannot afford to tolerate a status quo that denies a significant majority of God's people the right and privilege of responding to the full measure of God's call upon their lives, simply because of physiology. Prisoners rarely have the power to liberate themselves. Male guardians of the "sacred flame" of gospel preaching must die out to their own lust for power and dominance and become aggressively proactive in attacking prejudicial mind-sets, in challenging restrictive structures, and in confronting the inertia of a deeply entrenched discriminatory patriarchal system. There are four fronts, in particular, where the issue must be raised and the battle pressed on behalf of equal opportunity for women in church ministry.

BIBLICAL EMANCIPATION

There were many scrolls of Hebrew Scriptures that could have been handed to Jesus on that day when He stood up to read in the Nazareth synagogue, but divine providence dictated that it would be the Book of Isaiah. There were many powerful passages from which He could have preached His first sermon: some thundering forth with dire warnings about the wrath of God ready to exterminate sinners, others eloquently prophesying the coming of the Messiah of God. But no; He deliberately searched until He "found the place where it was written: 'The Spirit of the Lord is upon me, because he has anointed me to bring good news to the poor. He has sent me to **proclaim**

release to the captives and recovery of **sight to the blind,** to **let the oppressed go free,** to **proclaim the year of the Lord's favor'"** (Luke 4:17-18, emphasis added).

There are many ways in which the Bible can be read, interpreted, and used. It can become an instrument of condemnation, as it was for the law-obsessed Jews of Jesus' and Paul's time. It has been used to forge chains that have bound whole races and generations of people into the "vile institution of slavery," as John Wesley called it. It is being used by evangelical submissionists as a billy club to beat married women into mindless, dehumanizing subservience to their husbands. And it continues to be used as a "swift and terrible sword" to cut down women who would dare approach the sacred precincts of the pulpit.

William David Spencer tells about his wife, Aida, who though not having been reared in an evangelical family, blithely went off to seminary soon after becoming a Christian, to learn more about Jesus. While sitting in the Princeton Seminary cafeteria at a table full of evangelical brothers one day, she was accosted with this challenge, "What are you doing in seminary when women aren't suppose to speak?" All she had said, up to that point, was "Hello." They laughed it off and went on to other topics. Aida was stunned. In her five years as a Christian, she had never heard 1 Cor. 14:34-35 applied to her. Aida's husband relates her response: "What troubled her was the implied challenge that women had no right to learn in seminary. Such a conclusion seemed to strike at the very core of all that Christianity had revealed itself to be to her. Was not Jesus engaged in making all believers his disciples?"[3]

This launched her on a quest to master the New Testament in its original language, in order to resolve the dilemma of how Paul could write instructions prohibiting women from speaking or teaching in church and yet surround himself with so many women whom he warmly commends as "fellow workers in Christ Jesus" (Rom. 16:3, NASB). The result was a landmark work of careful exegesis upon which this defense of women preachers has relied heavily, *Beyond the Curse.*[4] Looking at the well-worn texts through a woman's eyes has yielded insights that even the most sympathetic of male exegetes would probably not have noticed.

The time has come for all of us to repent of turning the Scriptures into a "letter [that] kills" (2 Cor. 3:6). Most women engaged in professional ministry—past and present—testify to constant harassment by those who assault them with Bible verses. Certainly, there is no "letter" that has wounded them—even "killed" their resolve to follow God's call—more than the Pauline texts we have examined in some depth. Instead of binding women in chains forged from atomized and decontextualized scripture verses, we must aggressively preach the gospel of the "Spirit of life in Christ Jesus," which *sets them free* "from the law of sin and of death" (Rom. 8:2).

From Genesis to Revelation the Bible celebrates God's "Emancipation Proclamation" for all peoples from sin, death, and all that would diminish their lives. It rejoices in the human beings—male and female—created in freedom under God. It weeps over their freedom lost in the Garden of Eden. It does not shrink from recording the oppressive, enslaving, and destructive consequences of sin. It exults in a God who will not let sin and death have the last word but who intervenes redemptively, as early as Genesis 3, in forgiving sins, binding up the brokenhearted, clothing the naked, and setting captives free. It rises to its highest peaks in the Exodus event under the old covenant, and the death-resurrection of Christ in the new. Not only does it proclaim that "the truth will make you free," but Jesus declares that "if the Son makes you free, you will be free indeed" (John 8:32, 36).

While the Bible candidly acknowledges and faithfully records, on almost every page, that "the whole creation groans and suffers the pains of childbirth together until now," yet it anticipates that glorious day when "the creation itself also will be **set free from its slavery** to corruption into the freedom of the glory of the children of God" (Rom. 8:22, 21, NASB, emphasis added)—female as well as male children of God. The Bible was written, not to oppress but to liberate, not to discourage but to encourage, not to enslave but to emancipate. If we are to ever witness the healing of the seismic split that continues to divide the Church along gender lines, more than passive quietism is called for. We must take the initiative, seize the Scriptures even as Jesus did, and deliberately proclaim that which we believe to be its central, overarching, and fundamental message: namely, that of "good news" about God's acceptance of women on an equal footing with men; that of "release to the captives," women so long enslaved by men; that of "recovery of sight to the blind"—men blinded by the egoism of male-dominance and women blinded by truncated submissionism texts; that of setting free those God-called and Spirit-filled women who have been so callously and cruelly "oppressed"; and, finally, that of "proclaim[ing] the year of the Lord's favor" upon all of His handmaidens under the dispensation of the Holy Spirit.

Rena Yocom tells about a pastor's widow who answered a congregation's call to become their new pastor when her husband died, attending seminary while pastoring. A plumber's services were needed at the parsonage. The young apprentice asked the woman whether her husband was the preacher. "No, I am," she said. The plumber was shocked: "Don't you know that Paul told women to be silent in church?" Gently, the pastor replied, "Bless you, child. Paul didn't call me. God did!" That woman was

Leontine Kelley, who went on to become a bishop in the United Methodist church.[5]

ENLARGING OUR VISION OF GOD

God himself may have said, "I am God and not man" (Hos. 11:9, NASB), but it is hard for us to imagine Him as anything other than male. God as "Father" conveys images of masculinity, sovereignty, and patriarchy. These are dominant in the Scriptures, deeply engraved upon the human psyche, and exceedingly difficult to dislodge.

It is a truism that people tend to become like the gods they serve. This is certainly the case in considering the matter of God's gender and the issue of women preachers. If God has revealed himself (not herself) as our Heavenly Father (not Mother), if Jesus was truly incarnate as a man (not a woman), and if we hold that "in him [not her] the whole fullness of deity dwells bodily" (Col. 2:9), then it would seem to follow that He is more transparently and exactly represented before the congregation of God's people by males than by females.

Admitting the power of words, especially personal pronouns, to form deep and evocative concepts of God, we must nevertheless face the limits of language and its analogies. For instance, if the fact that Jesus was incarnate as a male human being indicates that God is male as opposed to female, then why shouldn't we affirm that God is a Jew as opposed to a Gentile? Furthermore, if the Church is the "bride of Christ," then why shouldn't it follow that women ought to have the predominance since they more exactly reflect the true gender and nature of the Church?

We must steadfastly resist making too much of anthropomorphic images of God in the Scriptures, for "God is spirit, and those who worship him must worship in spirit and truth" (John 4:24). He is neither male nor female but beyond all gender differentiation. Thus, to literalize figurative descriptions of God is both heretical and idolatrous.

On the other hand, we must also avoid the opposite error of not taking seriously the manifold ways in which God has chosen to reveal himself through language images and symbols in the Scriptures. If God was to disclose himself as a "person" and not a "thing" or "force," it was necessary that He squeeze himself into the narrow framework of human concepts, with all of its limitations, including gender specificity. While many ancient cultures were able to conceive of—and worship—a mother-goddess, that was an impossibility for the Israelites, especially given the patriarchal structure of their families and tribal lives.

It is true that the Bible does employ mostly male pronouns, metaphors, and images in speaking of God. Yet this is not exclusively the case. For instance, God sews, clothes, and cooks food—strictly a woman's work in biblical times (Gen. 3:21; Exod. 16:4; Neh. 9:21). God conceives, births, and suckles His children—all exclusively female roles (Isa. 42:14-16; 45:9-10; 46:3-4). He is even described as the perfect midwife (Ps. 22:9; 71:6). When the Israelites think that God has abandoned them in exile, He asks, "Can a woman forget her nursing child, or show no compassion for the child of her womb?" (Isa. 49:15). David speaks of the profound rest he experiences when he trusts God "like a child quieted at its mother's breast" (Ps. 131:2, RSV). To the returned exiles God promises: "As a mother comforts her child, so I will comfort you; you shall be comforted in Jerusalem" (Isa. 66:13). Isaiah 40—66 is heavily laced with mothering metaphors.

Fathers may leave nurturing young children to mothers, but not God. "It was I who taught Ephraim to walk, . . . I bent down to them and fed them" (Hos. 11:3-4). God compares himself, in His protective care of His people, to a mother eagle that "stirs up its nest, and hovers over its young; as it spreads its wings, takes them up, and bears them aloft on its pinions" (Deut. 32:11). Likewise, Jesus utilizes a mothering metaphor when He cries in anguish, "O Jerusalem, Jerusalem . . . How often I wanted to gather your children together, the way a hen gathers her chicks under her wings, and you were unwilling" (Matt. 23:37, NASB). As a lioness and mother bear feeds and protects its young, so does God guard and provide for His people (Isa. 31:4; Hos. 13:8; Lam. 3:10-11).

It is apparent that God himself ignored man-defined conventions and revealed himself, numerous times and in many ways, through the use of female pronouns, symbols, and analogies. This underscores something we noted earlier about the original creation of human beings in His own image as "male and female": namely, there is something in the character and nature of God that corresponds to the woman as fully as to the man. Conversely, there are unique and vital dimensions of God that can be disclosed more transparently and authentically through females than males. Aida Spencer puts it succinctly:

> If the Bible uses feminine imagery to mirror certain aspects of God, should not the church allow women leaders to reflect God similarly? For God is like mothers and like females in that God has the capacity to bear burdens, to produce life, to save, to perform the inexplicable, to be decisive, to be thorough and careful, to be constant, to be compassionate, to calm, to comfort, to care, to protect, to help, to love, to bring joy, to command fear and immediate response, to intimidate, to destroy, to guide, to educate, to feed, to persevere, to develop, to rule, and to be merciful. . . . The church indeed will be "happy" if it follows our God, freeing woman from the curse of the evil tree to become the fruitful tree of life God intends her to be.[6]

Amalie Shannon expresses the frustration and hope of women ministers everywhere when she writes about the need of the church to enlarge its vision of God: "Weary of expending our energies on efforts to be recognized, we covet a theology that embraces all humanity on the same level of grace. Our vision for women emerging into new roles in our church is one in which God's will is that we, women and men, are one in Christ Jesus."[7]

God, as He is in himself, lies far beyond the stretch of human imagination and the boundaries of descriptive language. If we must speak of Him in gender-specific terms— and we must since the Scriptures do, then let us be careful not to squeeze Him into our narrow, biased, and prejudicial mold to where He is perceived as favoring one gender above another. Even after Pentecost, Peter persisted in an inherited and deeply ingrained loathing of all Gentiles, particularly the hated Roman oppressors. While praying on a rooftop in Joppa, however, he had a startling vision that shattered his racial prejudice. His vision of God was so enlarged that he exclaimed, in the house of Cornelius, a despised Roman centurion no less, "I most certainly understand now that God is not one to show partiality" (Acts 10:34, NASB). If God deals graciously and impartially with Jew and Gentile, then why not female and male as well? While thankful for the gift of language and the ways in which it discloses God's character and nature to us, we must, ultimately, bow with the apostle Paul and confess, "O the depth of the riches and wisdom and knowledge of God! How unsearchable are his judgments and how inscrutable his ways! . . . For from him and through him and to him are all things. To him be the glory forever. Amen" (Rom. 11:33, 36).

WOMEN PREACHERS AND RADICAL FEMINISTS

It must be candidly admitted that forces unleashed by the equal rights movement have been part of the mix of complex sociological and cultural factors contributing to the destabilization of society's primal institution, the family. Having gained access to an education, the political process, and a strong foothold in the work force, women have acquired an independence never before enjoyed. Equal rights has laid an axe at the roots of the patriarchal family with its clearly delineated hierarchy and sharply defined roles. It has empowered women to take their lives and destinies into their own hands. Wives no longer are forced to remain in an abusive or dehumanizing marriage. Men often experience crises of identity in the face of assertive and successful females, both in the workplace and at home. The problems caused by this upheaval—particularly as they impinge upon the family—are real, urgent, and not likely to go away soon. But the existence of these problems does not nullify the validity of women's God-given aspirations.

We must face the fact that all freedom movements in history have been disruptive. The liberation of the children of Israel from slavery left Egypt devastated and bankrupt. The gospel of freedom from the tyranny of the law, won by Jesus and preached by Paul, precipitated a rupture within the covenant community of God's people that has yet to be healed. Martin Luther's reformation, setting Christians free from the tyranny of works righteousness, led not only to a seismic fracture in the monolithic Roman Catholic church but also to the scandalous proliferation of Christian denominations and sects. The high-minded, biblically based, evangelically driven crusade to set slaves free embroiled the United States in its bloodiest conflict ever and nearly destroyed the Union. The civil rights struggle divided our nation as no other issue in this century. The current right-to-life movement is tearing apart families, dividing churches, and inflaming communities as no other issue. Freedom movements call into question the status quo, challenge entrenched traditions, and have always upset the equilibrium.

Yet what is the alternative? Dictatorship? Slavery? Bondage? The domination of the weak by the strong? Back to the "good old days" of rigid patriarchy where families were more stable but women less free? And less human? Families where fathers exercised absolute power over their children and could slap, whip, beat, and kill their offspring with impunity? Or sell them into slavery, or expel them from the family (as Abraham did with Ishmael), or even offer them up to their gods as blood sacrifices (as Abraham almost did and Manasseh succeeded in doing)?

History teaches that while freedom destabilizes, it also generates unimaginable new possibilities. From Egypt's ashes came the covenant people of God. Out of fractured Judaism emerged Christianity. Beyond the upheaval that tore apart the monolithic and autocratic Catholic church came a reformed, revitalized, and democratized Body of Christ in which diversity has proven to be one of its most positive assets. From the blood, flame, and smoke of our young country's conflagration over slavery, and the subsequent civil rights upheaval, has arisen a nation that is stronger, richer, and nobler. And out of the equal rights movement we are beginning to see quality, love-bonded marriages emerge that have enriched family life—not to mention a focused concern for the education and welfare of children unprecedented in human history.

Why, then, shouldn't we expect to see arise, out of the current ferment over women's full participation in ministry, an entirely new dimension of spiritual vitality and church renewal? We have already had a taste of it in the

19th- and early 20th-century evangelical equal rights movement. It would be hard to argue that the cause of Christ has been retarded or irreparably damaged because of women preachers. To the contrary, one can only wonder what today's evangelical and holiness churches might look like—not to mention the world missions enterprise—if the venturesome and courageous women preachers of an earlier generation had succumbed to the letter of the law and kept silent. We do not have to look far to see what might happen if we dare to unchain God-called and Spirit-filled women and set them free. Let us consider one notable 20th-century example.

Henrietta Mears reigned for 35 years as the dean of evangelical women, and she wielded unprecedented influence from her position as director of Christian education at Hollywood Presbyterian Church (1928-63). She has been credited with doing more to dignify the work of Sunday Schools than any other person in history. Though she neither sought nor received ordination, she nevertheless became one of the most popular and widely traveled Bible teachers and preachers of her generation. She authored over a dozen widely circulated books and numerous Bible study series.

She exercised phenomenal leadership initiative by launching more organizations than any other evangelical leader. She founded the National Sunday School Association, started the Greater Los Angeles Sunday School Association, established Forest Home Christian Conference Center, inaugurated Gospel Light Publications, initiated GLINT—a missionary organization formed to translate and distribute Christian publications around the world—and was the prime mover behind the Hollywood Christian Association, which has made an incalculable impact for Christ upon the entertainment communities.

In addition to the thousands who committed their lives to Christ, over 400 men and women were called into full-time Christian service under her ministry. The list includes such notable evangelical leaders as Bill Bright, founder of Campus Crusade for Christ; Jim Rayburn of Young Life; Dr. Irwin Moon of Moody's Institute of Science; Richard C. Halverson, who for decades has wielded enormous influence as pastor of Fourth Presbyterian Church in Washington, D.C.; Don Moomow, former UCLA All-American football player and now highly respected pastor of the Bel Aire Presbyterian Church; Rafer Johnson, Olympic decathlon champion; Dick Halverson of World Vision; Paul Carlson, medical missionary whose martyrdom in Africa inspired hundreds of others to take up the cause of world missions; and many more.

Billy Graham sought out Henrietta for counsel on how to be filled with the Holy Spirit prior to his historic 1949 Los Angeles Crusade. While at Forest Home he fought the spiritual battle of his life. He recalls, "I remember walking down a trail, trampling alone in the world, almost wrestling with God. I dueled with my doubts, and my willingness to be centered in the cross-fire. Finally, in desperation, I surrendered my will to the living God as revealed in Scripture. Within six weeks we started the Los Angeles Crusade and the rest is history."[8] He testifies that she has had more influence upon his life than any other person, apart from his mother and wife.

In the bosom of the entertainment world's capital—"sin city"—God raised up a woman who would, more than any other individual in the mid-20th century, enhance the cause of Christ across denominational lines through what has been broadly called the evangelical movement. One wonders what today's church would look like if this Spirit-filled and enormously gifted woman—an authentic example of a "biblical feminist"—had been prohibited from exercising her ministry in full measure solely on the basis of gender.

EXERCISING THE "BARNABAS" PRINCIPLE

Unlike the secular arenas of work and politics, professional ministry in the church is carried out "by invitation only." Jesus did not take it upon himself to enter into the stream of humanity: God sent Him. Neither did He suddenly appear in Galilee and get on with preaching. He waited for a fitting introduction by John the Baptist and an appropriate ordination by the Holy Spirit following His baptism. The disciples did not volunteer to become apostles but were deliberately called, trained, and then sent out. They did not seize authority to preach but were commissioned by Jesus.

We may never have heard of Saul of Tarsus had not Barnabas, pastor of the church at Antioch, sought him out and invited him to participate in his ministry. The first missionary movement, which transformed Christianity from an obscure Jewish sect into the major world religion that it is today, may never have occurred if the church at Antioch had not fasted, prayed, and then given their official blessing to Paul and Barnabas through the laying on of hands before sending them on their way to preach to the Gentiles. Likewise, if Barnabas and Peter had not reached out and made a place of service for young John Mark, the church's first "missionary dropout," the Gospel of Mark may never have been written, nor Matthew and Luke who borrowed heavily from its contents. No wonder Barnabas was called "son of encouragement" (Acts 4:36).

Likewise, not much is going to happen to set women free until local church leaders, pastors, and denominational officials aggressively reach out and invite them to participate more actively in public ministry. It is just as unreasonable to expect that women preachers, teachers, educators, theologians, and leaders will emerge, entirely on their own, full grown and mature—like bumblebees— as to imagine that male ministers come that way. All God-called and Spirit-filled potential ministers are "dead in the water" until someone in a position of authority recognizes their gifts, invites them to participate in increasingly responsible forms of ministry, supports them in times of challenge, and encourages them along the way. It is only by active involvement in ministry that natural gifts can be developed, skills learned, experience gained, and potential actualized. The attention and nurture we so readily extend to our male professional ministry aspirants must be extended to our women as well. Since there are so few role models for women in public ministry, this whole process will have to be shepherded with uncommon dedication and extraordinary effort. It will have to be coupled with a teaching ministry to the church, helping congregations face and transcend their inherited antipathy toward women, and be ready to accept them in positions of public ministry and leadership.

One way to begin this process is to democratize worship and deliberately include women in all aspects of church work and administration. Why not women ushers as well as men? And women included among those who serve Holy Communion? Why not encourage greater participation of women on church boards and councils—a not unreasonable objective considering the fact that most of the real work of the church is done by women? Is God offended if an invocation or pastoral prayer is lifted in a feminine voice among the congregation of His people? Are holy Scriptures desecrated if handled and read by a woman? Since women are welcomed as church musicians and soloists, why not as ministers of music? In that people have grown accustomed to hearing prime-time news from female reporters, receiving instruction from female teachers and professors, healing from the hands of women doctors, representation by female attorneys and politicians, then why not women worship leaders and preachers? Like all innovations, it might take some getting used to, but aren't the potential benefits in terms of evangelism and enrichment infinitely worth the effort?

When vacancies occur on pastoral staffs, why not search for the best qualified person to fill the position, whether male or female? Does this not, however, raise the delicate issue of men and women working closely together as a pastoral team? Not any more so than male pastors working with female secretaries.

If women begin to emerge in church leadership and public ministry, isn't there a danger that they might displace men? Not any more so than when younger or more qualified leaders and ministers displace older and less productive men. What opening the doors to women offers is the opportunity for the church's ministry to multiply its redemptive impact because of more laborers in the harvest. Furthermore, women bring to the church not only a unique way of communicating divine truth but a whole different leadership style. Kathleen Hurty points out how Mary, the mother of Jesus, may serve as a prototype for women ministers: "Hers is a model marked by her experience of poverty, her willingness to be vulnerable, her deliberation and decision-making, her reliance on the Holy Spirit, her doubt, and her delight. These are marks of partnership . . . Partnership with God and with one another excludes the practices of domination and subordination. God's mercy is not passed down from a hierarchical pinnacle but bestowed by God's presence with us where we are."[9]

Monika Hellwig adds that the exclusion of women in past ages may actually equip them to be more effective ministers in the future. She suggests that because women have for the most part been excluded from roles of dominance in the churches, it may well be that they have learned a more characteristically Christian approach to the task of leadership—patterns of horizontal leadership or true ministry, leadership by the evoking of consensus, community building in the wisdom of the Holy Spirit. . . . Such a position also provides protection against arguments based on the authority of office that are not also based on the authority of experience and faithful listening to the experience of others. Moreover, one who speaks from a position of exclusion is more likely to speak on behalf of the excluded and is more likely to speak out of compassion.[10]

Women comprise the largest group of underutilized potential ministerial work force in the church. Nearly half of all American adults are single (46 percent), and the majority of these are women. Even among the married, only a minority are actively engaged in full-time mothering of small children at any given time. Is it fair to deny a woman an opportunity to develop her gifts and pursue a calling that would actualize her own unique individual potential if she is unmarried? Or childless? Or has children who are grown and gone? Since the overwhelming majority of women in the church fall into one of these categories, does it make sense to exclude them from professional and lay ministries by forcing them into a traditional wife-mother-homemaker mold that simply does not apply?

Again, we do not have to look far in order to see what might happen if we dare to unleash women for the full range of ministry in the church. Dr. Paul Cho, pastor of the world's largest church, tells about a revolutionary change in his thinking that occurred in his ministry. The church he founded in Seoul, South Korea, experienced rapid growth in its early years, but leveled out at about 3,000 members. He worked himself into such a state of nervous exhaustion that he was sidelined for several months. Out of this crisis experience came two insights that were to trigger the most explosive growth of any church in the history of Christianity.

The first had to do with small groups. Like John Wesley, he began to see unlimited potential for church growth if the church could be built upon a foundation of intimate, personalized, and dynamic cell groups where believers would be held accountable to each other for their own spiritual growth and evangelism. Through exercising the principle of "divide and grow" the church would increase, not by addition but by multiplication—which indeed it has done. His second insight had to do with women. Cho writes:

> God then showed me that we should use women as cell leaders. This was totally revolutionary to us, not only as conservative, Bible-believing Christians, but as Koreans. In Korea, as in most of the Orient, leadership is a man's business. The traditional role for women was to marry, have children, and keep a good and happy home. The husband is the provider and he is in complete control of his business and home life. Although we see things changing in Korea now, our culture still is basically male-oriented. So for women to be given positions of responsibility and authority in the church was more revolutionary than establishing the cell system itself.[11]

Then Cho relates how he had to work through, in his mind, the theological problem of how to interpret Paul's prohibitions regarding women speaking and teaching. However, he had to balance that over against Peter's Pentecost Day sermon in which both men and women were to preach under the anointing of the Holy Spirit. He also noted the many places where Paul encouraged female co-workers and fellow ministers in the preaching of the gospel and the work of the church. As he considered the fact that the first preachers of Christ's resurrection were women, and that nowhere did Jesus discriminate against them in any way, he says that

> I decided to use women as cell leaders in my church. Once the women began to be used and we had overcome all of the ensuing obstacles . . . the men in the church became much more cooperative. In all of the years I have been teaching the cell system, I found that my female associates have been loyal and reliable. They have not rebelled and done their own thing, but have worked hard.
>
> My advice to you then is, "Don't be afraid of using women."[12]

Paul Cho is leading the way in showing the entire church world that there is nothing to be afraid of in setting women free to minister on an equal footing with men. His church has long since passed the half-million mark in membership and shows no signs of leveling off.

CONCLUSION

We have reached a crisis point in the Wesleyan-Arminian holiness tradition. We are in danger of losing a major dimension of our spiritual and social heritage. We have allowed a strident fundamentalist and traditionalist force in our contemporary church world, which perpetuates the scandal of blatant sexist discrimination against women, to intimidate us and squeeze us into its narrow mold.

The choice before us is straightforward and urgent: Are we going to order our lives, as the people of God, under the dispensation of the curse where male domination and female subordination is the rule, or are we going to risk living in the freedom of the grace in which there is "no longer male and female; for all of you are one in Christ Jesus"? (Gal. 3:28). Are we going to live under the oppressive bondage of the law whereby gifted, God-called, and Spirit-filled women are forbidden to exercise their vocation simply because of gender—to the great loss of God's kingdom —or are we going to dare to live in the liberty of the Spirit where both men and women may hear and respond to the call of God to preach and where all may exercise their spiritual gifts for the edification of the Body of Christ and the evangelization of the world? How can we preach a glorious gospel of freedom from sin and yet tolerate keeping our God-called women in chains?

If the secular world sees the value of women and has learned to trust them in virtually all areas of service and leadership, can we as God-freed, God-filled Kingdom dwellers continue in such a God-dishonoring manner? Should we not bear uncompromised witness to the freedom of Christ by encouraging women to preach and teach, by soliciting (and heeding) their advice and expertise on church and denominational boards? How can we persist in demeaning the witness of grace by this kind of dehumanizing and debasing discrimination against our mothers, wives, daughters, and sisters in Christ—those choice and chosen persons whom God created in His own image and for whom Christ died? Can we continue to countenance a spirit of passive resistance that effectively blocks women from actualizing their God-given and Spirit-anointed call?

NOTES

Chapter 1

1. Most of this information was provided in a telephone interview (Sept. 26, 1991) with Mary Zimmer, executive director of Southern Baptist Women in Ministry, 2800 Frankfurt Ave., Louisville, KY 40206.

2. Diane Cunningham, *New Horizons* (Kansas City: Church of the Nazarene, Pastoral Ministries Dept.), June 1991.

3. *Manual, Church of the Nazarene* (Kansas City: Nazarene Publishing House, 1980), 904.10.

4. These statistics are for 1992 and represent only the Churches of the Nazarene in the United States and Canada.

5. Juanita Evans Leonard, "Women, Change, and the Church," *Called to Minister, Empowered to Serve*, Juanita Evans Leonard, ed. (Anderson, Ind.: Warner Press, 1989), 152.

6. Rev. Elsie Wallace was appointed by Dr. Bresee to fill a vacancy in the superintendency of the Northwest District in 1920, and she served for several months until another superintendent could be elected at the following annual District Assembly.

7. Fannie McDowell Hunter's *Women Preachers* (Dallas, 1905) was the first and only book written by a Nazarene author defending the right of women to preach, according to Church of the Nazarene archivist, Stan Ingersol.

8. Edith L. Blumhofer, "Women in Evangelicalism and Pentecostalism," in *Women and Church*, Melanie A. May, ed. (Grand Rapids: Eerdmans Publishing Co., 1991), 6.

9. Joan Brown Campbell, "Toward a Renewed Community of Women and Men," *Women and Church*, 79.

10. Amalie R. Shannon, "A Lutheran Woman Looks at the Decades," *Women and Church*, 60-64.

11. Elizabeth Howell Verdesi, *In but Still Out* (Philadelphia: Westminster Press, 1973), 181, as cited in *Women and Church*, 101.

12. *Yearbook of American and Canadian Churches*, Constant H. Jaquet, ed. (Nashville: Abingdon, 1988), as cited in *Women and Church*, 107.

13. *Christianity Today* (Jan. 13, 1989), 40-41.

14. Ibid.

15. J. I. Packer, "Let's Stop Making Women Presbyters," *Christianity Today* (Feb. 11, 1991), 20.

16. Alan Gallay, "The Great Awakening," *Masters and Slaves in the House of the Lord*, John B. Boles, ed. (Louisville, Ky.: University Press of Kentucky, 1988), chap. 1.

17. H. Shelton Smith, Robert T. Handy, and Lefferts A. Loetscher, *American Christianity* (New York: Scribners, 1963), 2:177, as cited in Patricia Gundry, *Woman, Be Free* (Grand Rapids: Zondervan Publishing Company, 1979), 51.

18. Ibid., 185, cited in ibid., 52.

19. Clarence L. Mohr, "Slaves and White Churches in Confederate Georgia," *Masters and Slaves*, 153.

20. Editorial, *Christianity Today* (Oct. 4, 1985), 18.

21. *The Works of John Wesley*, Frank Baker, ed. (Oxford: Clarendon Press, 1982), 26:158.

22. John Wesley, *Explanatory Notes upon the New Testament* (London: Epworth Press, 1950), 570.

23. Jack B. Rogers and Donald K. McKim, *The Authority and Interpretation of the Bible* (San Francisco: Harper and Row, 1979), 77-78.

Chapter 2

1. Gundry, *Woman, Be Free*, 17.

2. George Barrington [pseud.], *The History of New South Wales*, 17, cited by Robert Hughes, *The Fatal Shore* (New York: Random House, 1988), 15.

3. Ibid., 16.

4. Ibid.

5. Farley Mowat, *Tundra* (Toronto: McClelland and Stewart, 1977), 40.

6. Plato, *The Republic*, W. H. D. Rouse, trans. (New York: Mentor, 1956), 456.

7. Susan G. Bell, *Women: From the Greeks to the French Revolution* (Belmont, Calif.: Wadsworth Publishing Company, 1973), 18, cited in Gundry, *Woman, Be Free*, 18.

8. Aristotle, *Politics*, trans. *Oxford University, The Basic Works of Aristotle*, Richard McDean, ed. (New York: Random House, 1941), 1:1254B, as cited in John Temple Bristow, *What Paul Really Said About Women* (San Francisco: Harper, 1988), 6.

9. Marabel Morgan, *The Total Woman* (Old Tappan, N.J.: Fleming H. Revell, 1973), 80.

10. Xenophon, "Within the Home," *The Greek Reader*, A. L. Wholl, trans. (New York: Doubleday, 1943), 625. (As quoted in Bristow, *What Paul Really Said*, 7.)

11. Ibid.

12. Bristow, *What Paul Really Said*, 7.

13. The primary source for the status and role of women in Judaism is Joachim Jeremias, *Jerusalem in the Time of Jesus* (Philadelphia: Fortress Press, 1969), 359-76. It is instructive to note that this chapter, "The Social Position of Women," is not part of the main work but is included in the Appendix. Even as recently as 1969, a major European New Testament scholar is not willing to include his chapter on women as part of the main body of his book!

Also providing valuable source material on the status and role of women in first-century Judaism are Virginia Ramey Mollenkott, *Women, Men, and the Bible* (New York: Crossroad, 1988), 2-22; Bristow, *What Paul Really Said*, 14-29; and the *Jewish Encyclopedia*, Isidore Singer, ed. (New York: Funk and Wagnalls, 1905), 12:556-59.

14. *The Secret Teachings of Jesus*, Marvin W. Meyer, trans. (New York: Random House, 1986), Codex II, 51.

15. Elaine Pagels, *The Gnostic Gospels* (New York: Random House, 1981), 72.

16. Ibid., 61.

17. Ibid., 62.

18. Ibid., 72.

19. Pagels, *The Gnostic Gospels*, 76.

20. Susan G. Bell, *Women*, as cited in Gundry, *Woman, Be Free*, 22.

21. Ibid., 18, as cited in Gundry, *Woman, Be Free*, 18.

22. Annie Machisale-Muscopole, "Toward a New Ecumenical Movement: A Malawian Perspective," May, *Women and Church*, 141 ff.

23. Ibid., 149.

24. Paul K. Jewett, *The Ordination of Women* (Grand Rapids: Eerdmans Publishing Co., 1980), 103.

25. Elise Boulding, *The Underside of History* (Boulder, Colo.: Westview Press, 1976).

26. Ibid., 37.

27. Ibid., 38.

Chapter 3

1. As cited by Aida Besancon Spencer, *Beyond the Curse* (New York: Thomas Nelson, 1985), 18.

2. Cited by Spencer, *Beyond the Curse*, 19.

3. Ibid.

4. See, for instance, feminine divine imagery in Isa. 46:3-4; 63:9; Exod. 19:4; Deut. 32:18.

5. Mary Hayter, *The New Eve in Christ* (Grand Rapids: Eerdmans Publishing Co., 1987), 39.

6. Spencer, *Beyond the Curse*, 22.

7. See Gerhard von Rad, *Old Testament Theology*, D. M. G. Stalker, trans. (New York: Harper and Row, 1962), 1:149-50.

8. Donald E. Gowan, *From Eden to Babel* (Grand Rapids: Eerdmans Publishing Co., 1988), 48.

9. Spencer, *Beyond the Curse*, 30.

10. Cited by Richard N. Longenecker, "Authority, Hierarchy, and Leadership Patterns in the Bible," *Women, Authority, and the Bible*, Alvera Michelsen, ed. (Downers Grove, Ill.: InterVarsity Press, 1986), 69-70.

11. Julia O'Faolain and Lauro Martines, eds., *Not in God's Image* (New York: Harper and Row, 1973), 132, cited in Gundry, *Woman, Be Free*, 20.

12. Ibid., 31.

13. Ibid.

14. Ibid., 35-36.

15. Gretchen Gaebelein Hull, *Equal to Serve* (Old Tappan, N.J.: Fleming H. Revell, 1987), 87.

16. For a thorough listing and description of great women throughout Israel's history, see Herbert Lockyer, *All the Women of the Bible* (Grand Rapids: Zondervan, 1967).

17. Arlene Swidler, "In Search of Huldah," *The Bible Today* (Nov. 1978), 1783.

Chapter 4

1. See Constance F. Parvey, "The Theology and Leadership of Women in the New Testament," *Religion and Sexism*, Rosemary Radford Ruether, ed. (New York: Simon and Schuster, 1974), 139-46; Mary Rose D'Angelo, "Women in Luke-Acts," *Journal of Biblical Literature*, 109/3 (1990), 441-61; Letha Scanzoni and Nancy Hardesty, *All We're Meant to Be* (Waco, Tex.: Word, 1974), 215-16.

Chapter 5

1. Bristow, *What Paul Really Said*, 1.

2. Don Williams, *The Apostle Paul and Women in the Church* (Ventura, Calif.: Gospel Light, 1980).

3. See Spencer, *Beyond the Curse*, 115-16, for a thorough linguistic study of these two words.

4. Williams, *Apostle Paul*, 45.

5. Ibid., 54.

6. *The Analytical Greek Lexicon* (New York: Harper), 354.

7. Bristow, *What Paul Really Said*, 85-87.

8. Ibid., 86.

9. Ibid., 88.

10. Virginia Ramey Mollenkott, *Women, Men, and the Bible* (New York: Crossroad, 1988), 79-82.

11. Klyne R. Shodgrass, "Galatians 3:28: Conundrum or Solution?" *Women, Authority, and the Bible*, 174.

12. Ibid., 180.

13. Ibid., 82.

14. Susie C. Stanley, *Women, Authority, and the Bible*, 186.

15. Luther Lee, "Woman's Right to Preach the Gospel," *Five Sermons and a Tract by Luther Lee*, Donald W. Dayton, ed. (Chicago: Holrad House, 1975), 80-81; cited in Stanley, *Women, Authority, and the Bible*, 183.

16. Ibid., 185.

17. Ibid., 187-88.

18. Helen Andelin, *Fascinating Womanhood* (Santa Barbara, Calif.: Pacific Press, 1965), 57.

19. Morgan, *The Total Woman*, 80.

20. Bristow, *What Paul Really Said*, 38.

21. For a more complete exegesis of Eph. 5:21-22 see ibid., 38-41.

22. Mollenkott, *Women*, 92.

23. For a thorough study of the usage of *kephale* in both the Old Testament Greek Septuagint and in the Greek New Testament, see Berkeley and Alvera Michelsen's chapter, "What Does *Kephale* Mean in the New Testament?" in *Women, Authority, and the Bible*, 97-132.

24. The Song of Solomon does celebrate the love of a man for a woman, but nowhere identifies her as his wife. Hosea is directed to marry Gomer, a prostitute, as a living demonstration of God's love for His adulterous bride, Israel. Even though Hosea married her and took her back a second time, there is no indication that he actually loved her for her own sake. The only exception I can find is Elkanah, Samuel's father, who gave a double portion of his sacrifices to one of his wives, Hannah, "because he loved her, though the Lord had closed her womb" (1 Sam. 1:5). In that he had at least two wives, this still falls short of the Pauline model.

Chapter 6

1. See R. Scroggs, "Paul and the Eschatological Woman," *Journal of the American Academy of Religion* 40 (1972): 283-303; 42 (1974): 532-37.

2. *The Interpreter's Bible*, George Arthur Buttrick, ed. (Nashville: Abingdon Press, 1953), 10:213.

3. Ibid.

4. R. K. McGregor Wright, "A Response to the Danvers Statement," Part II, "Women Leaders in the New Testament," 4. An unpublished paper delivered to the Christians for Biblical Equality Conference, St. Paul, in 1989, and distributed by the same.

5. See Richard and Catherine Clark Kroeger, "Pandemonium and Silence at Corinth," *The Reformed Journal* (June 1988), 6-11. Also C. K. Barrett, *The New Testament Backgrounds* (New York: Harper and Row, 1966), chap. 6, "Mystery Religions"; Robert C. Grant, *A Historical Introduction to the New Testament* (New York: Harper and Row, 1963), 330.

6. For a more complete word study on these verses, see Bristow, *What Paul Really Said*, 61-66.

7. Walter L. Liefeld, "Women, Submission, and Ministry in 1 Corinthians," *Women, Authority, and the Bible*, 141-42.

8. Richard and Catherine Clark Kroeger, "May Women Teach? Heresy in the Pastoral Epistles" (unpublished paper that may be obtained from Christians for Biblical Equality, 380 Lafayette Freeway, Suite 122, St. Paul, MN 55107-1216). See also Richard and Catherine Clark Kroeger, *I Suffer Not a Woman: Rethinking I Timothy 2:11-15 in Light of Ancient Evidence* (Grand Rapids: Baker Book House, 1992).

9. Kroeger, "May Women Teach?"

10. Spencer, *Beyond the Curse*, 77.

11. Ibid., 80.

12. Ibid.

13. For a fuller treatment of the positions advanced, see Spencer, *Beyond the*

Curse, 71-91; and Bristow, *What Paul Really Said*, 67-75.

14. For an excellent introduction to the Nag Hammadi literature, see Pagels, *Gnostic Gospels*, and her more recent book, *Adam, Eve, and the Serpent* (New York: Random House, 1989). Also Marvin W. Meyer, *The Secret Teachings of Jesus* (New York: Random House, 1984). For a helpful summary of Eastern religious teachings and Gnostic myths that pertain to 1 Tim. 2:11-15, see two unpublished papers by Richard and Catherine Clark Kroeger titled "May Women Teach? Heresy in the Pastoral Epistles" and "Women Elders: Sinners or Servants?" (Distributed by Christians for Biblical Equality, 380 Lafayette Freeway, Suite 122, St. Paul, MN 55107-1216).

15. Pagels, *Adam, Eve, and the Serpent*, 68.

16. Ibid., 66.

17. Spencer, *Beyond the Curse*, 93.

18. Council on Biblical Manhood and Womanhood, "The Danvers Statement," *Christianity Today* (Jan. 13, 1989), 43-44.

19. Christians for Biblical Equality, "Men, Women & Biblical Equality," statement published in *Christianity Today* (Apr. 9, 1990), 36-37.

20. Ibid.

Chapter 7

1. Donald W. Dayton, *Discovering an Evangelical Heritage*, "The Evangelical Roots of Feminism" (New York: Harper and Row, 1976), 86.

2. Ibid.

3. Janette Hassey, *No Time for Silence* (Grand Rapids: Zondervan, 1986), xii.

4. Williston Walker, *A History of the Christian Church* (New York: Scribners, 1970), 421.

5. Barbara J. MacHaffie, *Her Story: Women in Christian Tradition* (Philadelphia: Fortress Press, 1986), 89.

6. Cited in Paul Wesley Chilcote, *John Wesley and the Women Preachers of Early Methodism* (Metuchen, N.J., and London: Scarecrow Press, 1991), 10.

7. Ruth A. Tucker and Walter L. Liefeld, *Daughters of the Church: Women and Ministry from New Testament Times to the Present* (Grand Rapids: Zondervan, 1987), 231.

8. MacHaffie, *Her Story*, 90.

9. Ibid., 90-91.

10. Chilcote, *John Wesley and the Women*, 57.

11. Cited in ibid., 121.

12. Ibid., 122.

13. See Earl Kent Brown, *Women of Mr. Wesley's Methodism* (New York: Edwin Mellon Press, 1983), 15-31.

14. Thomas M. Morrow, *Early Methodist Women* (London: Epworth Press, 1967), 14, as cited in an unpublished paper by Lucille Sider Dayton and Donald M. Dayton, "Women in the Holiness Movement" (Christians for Biblical Equality), n.d.

15. Chilcote, *John Wesley and the Women*, 182.

16. Brown, *Mr. Wesley's Methodism*, 219.

17. B. T. Roberts, *Ordaining Women* (Rochester, N.Y.: Earnest Christian Publishing House, 1891), 59, as cited in Dayton and Dayton, "Women in the Holiness Movement," 3.

18. Robert F. Wearmouth, *Methodism and the Common People of the Eighteenth Century* (London: Epworth Press, 1945), 223, as cited in Dayton and Dayton, ibid., 2 (emphasis added).

19. Tucker and Liefeld, *Daughters of the Church*, 274.

20. Dayton, *Discovering an Evangelical Heritage*, 90.

21. Edith Deen, *Great Women of the Christian Faith* (Westwood, N.J.: Barbour and Company, 1959), 377-78.

22. Asa Mahan, *Autobiography, Intellectual, Moral and Spiritual* (London: T. Woolmer, 1882), 169, as cited in Dayton and Dayton, "Women in the Holiness Movement," 4.

23. Deen, *Great Women of the Christian Faith*, 376-78.

24. Timothy L. Smith, *Called unto Holiness* (Kansas City: Nazarene Publishing House, 1962), 12, 23.

25. Rosemary Radford Ruether, Rosemary Skinner Keller, eds., *Women and Religion in America: Volume 1: The Nineteenth Century* (San Francisco: Harper and Row, 1981), 217-18.

26. Hassey, *No Time for Silence*, 11.

27. Ibid., 15-19.

28. Ibid., 31.

29. Ibid.

30. Dayton, *Discovering an Evangelical Heritage*, 91.

31. Susie Stanley, "Women Evangelists in the Church of God at the Beginning of the Twentieth Century," *Called to Minister, Empowered to Serve*, 38.

32. Dayton, *Discovering an Evangelical Heritage*, 98.

33. Ibid., 154.

34. Ibid., 155-56. Fannie McDowell Hunter's book, *Women Preachers*, was the first and only defense of women in ministry published by the denomination until this work. Strictly speaking, even hers was not produced by the Church of the Nazarene in that it was published before the 1908 union at Pilot Point.

35. Rebecca Laird, "The First Generation of Ordained Women in the Church of the Nazarene," Pacific School of Religion, an unpublished master of arts thesis (Berkeley, Calif.: 1990), iv and v.

36. James Blaine Chapman, "October Gleanings," *Herald of Holiness* (Oct. 15, 1930), 5.

37. Laird, "The First Generation," chap. 6.

38. William M. Greathouse, "Women in Ministry: An Editorial," *Herald of Holiness* (June 15, 1982), 1.

Chapter 8

1. For excellent surveys of women in Church history, see Elise Boulding, *The Underside of History: A View of Women Through Time;* Edith Deen, *Great Women of the Christian Faith;* Barbara J. MacHaffie, *Her Story: Women in Christian Tradition;* George H. Tavard, *Women in Christian Tradition;* and Ruth Tucker and Walter L. Liefeld, *Daughters of the Church.*

2. Rena M. Yocom, "Presents and Presence," *Women and Church,* Melanie May, ed. (Grand Rapids: Eerdmans, 1991), 70.

3. Spencer, *Beyond the Curse,* 141.

4. Ibid.

5. Yocom, *Women and Church,* 71.

6. Spencer, *Beyond the Curse,* 131.

7. Amalie R. Shannon, "A Lutheran Woman Looks at the Decades," *Women and Church,* 64.

8. Ethel May Baldwin and David V. Benson, *Henrietta Mears* (Glendale, Calif.: Gospel Light, 1966), 278-79.

9. Kathleen S. Hurty, "Ecumenical Leadership," *Women and Church,* 94-95.

10. Monika K. Hellwig, "Foreword," ibid., xii.

11. Paul Y. Cho, *More than Numbers* (Waco, Tex.: Word, 1984), 43-44.

12. Ibid.

BIBLIOGRAPHY

Standard Reference Works

The Analytical Greek Lexicon. New York: Harper, n.d.

Arndt, William F., and F. Wilbur Gingrich. *A Greek-English Lexicon of the New Testament.* Chicago: University of Chicago Press, 1957.

Kittel, Gerhard, and Gerhard Friedrich, eds. *Theological Dictionary of the New Testament.* Geoffrey W. Bromiley, trans. Abridged in one volume by Geoffrey W. Bromiley. Grand Rapids: Eerdmans, 1985.

Marshall, Alfred. *The Interlinear Greek-English New Testament.* London: Samuel Bagster and Sons, 1966.

Books

Andelin, Helen. *Fascinating Womanhood.* Santa Barbara, Calif.: Pacific Press, 1965.

Baker, Frank, ed. *The Works of John Wesley.* Oxford: Clarendon, 1982, Vol. 26.

Baldwin, Ethel May, and David V. Benson. *Henrietta Mears.* Glendale, Calif.: Gospel Light, 1966.

Barrett, C. K. *The New Testament Backgrounds.* New York: Harper, 1966.

Boles, John B., ed. *Master and Slaves in the House of the Lord.* Louisville, Ky.: University Press of Kentucky, 1988.

Boulding, Elise. *The Underside of History: A View of Women Through Time.* Boulder, Colo.: Westview, 1976.

Briscoe, Jill. *Women Who Changed Their World.* Wheaton, Ill.: Victor Books, Scripture Press, 1991.

Bristow, John Temple. *What Paul Really Said About Women.* San Francisco: Harper, 1988.

Brown, Earl Kent. *Women of Mr. Wesley's Methodism.* New York: Edwin Mellon Press, 1983.

Buttrick, George Arthur, ed. *The Interpreter's Bible.* Nashville: Abingdon, 1953. Vol. X.

Chilcote, Paul Wesley. *John Wesley and the Women Preachers of Early Methodism.* London: Scarecrow Press, 1991.

Cho, Paul. *More than Numbers.* Waco, Tex.: Word, 1984.

Dayton, Donald W. *Discovering an Evangelical Heritage.* San Francisco: Harper, 1976.

———, ed. *Holiness Tracts Defending the Ministry of Women.* New York: Garland, 1985.

Deen, Edith. *Great Women of the Christian Faith.* Westwood, N.J.: Barbour and Co., 1959.

Figes, Eva. *Patriarchal Attitudes*. New York: Stein and Day, 1970.

Gowan, Donald E. *From Eden to Babel*. Grand Rapids: Eerdmans, 1988.

Gundry, Patricia. *Neither Slave Nor Free*. San Francisco: Harper, 1987.

———. *Woman, Be Free*. Grand Rapids: Zondervan, 1977.

Hassey, Janette. *No Time for Silence*. Grand Rapids: Zondervan, 1986.

Hayter, Mary. *The New Eve in Christ*. Grand Rapids: Eerdmans, 1987.

Hollis, Harry N., et al., eds. *Christian Freedom for Women*. Nashville: Broadman, 1975.

Hull, Gretchen Gaebelein. *Equal to Serve*. Old Tappan, N.J.: Revell, 1987.

Hughes. *The Fatal Shores*. New York: Random House, 1988.

Jeremias, Joachim. *Jerusalem in the Time of Jesus*. Philadelphia: Fortress, 1969.

Jewett, Paul K. *The Ordination of Women*. Grand Rapids: Eerdmans, 1980.

Kroeger, Richard and Catherine. *Women Elders . . . Sinners or Servants?* New York: Council on Women and Church, United Presbyterian Church, USA, 1981.

———. *I Suffer Not a Woman: Rethinking I Timothy 2:11-15 in Light of Ancient Evidence*. Grand Rapids: Baker Book House, 1992.

Leonard, Juanita Evans, ed. *Called to Minister, Empowered to Serve*. Anderson, Ind.: Warner, 1989.

Loades, Ann, ed. *Feminist Theology: A Reader*. London: SPCK, 1990.

Lockyer, Herbert. *All the Women of the Bible*. Grand Rapids: Zondervan, 1967.

MacHaffie, Barbara J. *Her Story: Women in Christian Tradition*. Philadelphia: Fortress, 1986.

May, Melanie A., ed. *Women and Church*. Grand Rapids: Eerdmans, 1991.

Manual: Church of the Nazarene. Kansas City: Nazarene Publishing House, 1980.

Meyer, Marvin W., trans. *The Secret Teachings of Jesus*. New York: Random House, 1986.

Meyers, Carol. *Discovering Eve: Ancient Israelite Women in Context*. New York: Oxford University Press, 1988.

Michelsen, Alvera, ed. *Women, Authority, and the Bible*. Downers Grove, Ill.: InterVarsity, 1986.

Milhaven, Annie Lally. *Sermons Seldom Heard: Women Proclaim Their Lives*. New York: Crossroad, 1991.

Mollenkott, Virginia Ramey. *Women, Men, and the Bible*. New York: Crossroad, 1988.

Morgan, Marabel. *The Total Woman*. Old Tappan, N.J.: Fleming H. Revell, 1973.

Morrow, Thomas M. *Early Methodist Women*. London: Epworth, 1967.

Otwell, John H. *And Sarah Laughed*. Philadelphia: Westminster, 1977.

Pagels, Elaine. *Adam, Eve, and the Serpent*. New York: Random, 1988.

———. *The Gnostic Gospels*. New York: Random, 1989.

Plato. *The Republic*. W. H. D. Rouse, trans. New York: Mentor, 1956.

Rogers, Jack B., and Donald K. McKim. *The Authority and Interpretation of the Bible*. San Francisco: Harper, 1979.

Rothman, Sheila M. *Woman's Proper Place*. New York: Basic Books, 1978.

Ruether, Rosemary Radford, ed. *Religion and Sexism.* New York: Simon and Schuster, 1974.

Ruether, Rosemary Radford, and Rosemary Skinner Keller, eds. *Women and Religion in America.* San Francisco: Harper, 1981.

Scanzoni, Letha, and Nancy Hardesty. *All We're Meant to Be.* Waco, Tex.: Word, 1974.

Schaller, Lyle E. *Women as Pastors.* Nashville: Abingdon, 1982.

Smith, Timothy L. *Called unto Holiness.* Kansas City: Nazarene Publishing House, 1962.

Spencer, Aida Besancon. *Beyond the Curse: Women Called to Ministry.* New York: Thomas Nelson, 1985.

Stendahl, Krister. *The Bible and the Role of Women.* Philadelphia: Fortress, 1966.

Tavard, George H. *Woman in Christian Tradition.* Notre Dame, Ind.: Notre Dame Press, 1973.

Tucker, Ruth, and Walter L. Liefeld. *Daughters of the Church.* Grand Rapids: Zondervan, 1987.

Von Rad, Gerhard. *Old Testament Theology.* D. M. G. Stalker, trans. New York: Harper, 1962. Vol. I.

Walker, Williston. *A History of the Christian Church.* New York: Scribners, 1970.

Wearmouth, Robert F. *Methodism and the Common People of the Eighteenth Century.* London: Epworth, 1945.

Weidman, Judith L., ed. *Women Ministers.* San Francisco: Harper, 1981.

Wesley, John. *Explanatory Notes upon the New Testament.* London: Epworth, 1950.

Williams, Don. *The Apostle Paul and Women in the Church.* Ventura, Calif.: Gospel Light, 1980.